CLASSIC
QUILTS

CLASSIC QUILTS

TRADITION WITH A TWIST:
13 SENSATIONAL PATCHWORK & APPLIQUÉ PATTERNS

Rosemary Wilkinson, Editor

Intercourse, PA 17534
800/762-7171
www.GoodBooks.com

This edition copyright © 2008 by Good Books, Intercourse, PA 17534

International Standard Book Number: 978-1-56148-634-2
Library of Congress Catalog Card Number: 2008002133

Text, photography and illustrations © 2008 New Holland Publishers (UK) Ltd
Quilt designs copyright © 2008 Jane Coombes, Sarah Fincken, Nikki Foley, Janet Goddard,
Natalia Manley, Andrea McMillan, Karen Odinga and Gail Smith
Copyright © 2008 New Holland Publishers (UK) Ltd

Editorial Direction: Rosemary Wilkinson
Senior Editors: Naomi Walters & Emma Pattison
Designer: Zoe Mellors
Photography: Shona Wood
Illustrations: Carrie Hill
Templates: Stephen Dew
Production: Hazel Kirkman

Reproduction by Pica Digital PTE Ltd, Singapore
Printed and bound in Malaysia by Times Offset (M) Sdn Bhd

NOTE
The measurements for each project are given in imperial and metric. Use only one set of
measurements and do not interchange between them.

Library of Congress Cataloging-in-Publication Data:

Classic quilts : tradition with a twist : 13 sensational patchwork & appliqué patterns.
       p. cm.
   ISBN-13: 978-1-56148-634-2 (pbk. : alk. paper)
   1. Patchwork–Patterns. 2. Quilting–Patterns. 3. Appliqué–Patterns.
           TT835.C5935 2008
           746.46'041–dc22

       2008002133

CONTENTS

BASIC TOOLS AND TECHNIQUES

MATERIALS

PATCHWORK FABRICS

The easiest fabrics to work with for patchwork are closely woven, 100% cotton. They "cling" together, making a stable unit for cutting and stitching; they don't fray too readily and they press well. Quilting shops and suppliers stock a fantastic range in both solid colors and prints, usually in 45 in/115 cm widths. All of the quilts in this book are made using these cottons.

BACKING AND BINDING FABRICS

The backing and binding fabrics should be the same type and weight as the fabrics used in the patchwork top. They can be a coordinating color or a strong contrast. You could also be adventurous and piece the backing, too, to make a reversible quilt. In either case, the color of the binding needs to work with both the top and the backing fabric designs.

BATTING

Various types of batting are available in cotton, polyester, wool or mixed fibers. They can be bought in pre-cut sizes suitable for the different sizes of bed quilts or in specific lengths cut from a bolt. They also come in different weights or "lofts" depending on how padded you want the quilt to be. Lightweight polyester batting is the most commonly used, but some wool or cotton types are more suited to hand quilting. Some need to be closely quilted to prevent them from bunching up; others can be quilted up to 8 in/20 cm apart. If in doubt, follow the manufacturer's instructions.

QUANTITIES

The quantities given at the beginning of each project have been calculated to allow for a bit extra – just in case! A few of the quilts combine cutting down the length of the fabric with cutting across the width. This is to make the most economical use of fabric or to obtain border pieces cut in one piece.

Unless otherwise stated, any 10 in /25 cm requirement is the "long" quarter – the full width of the fabric – and not the "fat" quarter, which is a piece 18 x 22 in/50 x 56 cm.

PREPARATION

All fabrics should be washed prior to use in order to wash out any excess dye and to avoid fabrics shrinking at different rates. Wash each fabric separately and rinse – repeatedly if necessary – until the water is clear of any color run. If washing in a machine, cut a piece of white fabric from a larger piece. Place one piece in with the wash. After the wash, compare the white fabric with its other half. If they are the same, the fabric did not run. If a particular fabric continues to color the water no matter how many times it is washed/rinsed and you have your heart set on using it, try washing it together with a small piece of each of the fabrics you intend to use with it.

Below: Choosing fabrics in coordinating colors or strong contrasts will add to the beauty of your finished quilt.

If these fabrics retain their original colors, i.e. they match the pieces not washed with the offending fabric, you would probably be safe in using it. But if in doubt – don't!

Once washed and before they are completely dry, iron the fabrics and fold them selvage to selvage – as they were originally on the bolt – in preparation for cutting. Be sure to fold them straight so that the selvages line up evenly, even if the cut edges are not parallel (this will be fixed later).

THREADS

For machine quilting use lightweight or monofilament threads. For quilting by hand, use a thread labeled "quilting thread", which is heavier than normal sewing thread. Some threads are 100% cotton; others have a polyester core that is wrapped with cotton. You can use a thread either to match or to contrast with the fabric that is being quilted. Alternatively, use a variegated thread toning or contrasting with the patchwork. It is also acceptable to use several colors on the same piece of work. If the quilt is to be tied rather than quilted, use a heavier thread, such as perle cotton, coton à broder or stranded embroidery cotton.

EQUIPMENT

There are some essential pieces of equipment that have revolutionized the making of patchwork quilts. Rotary cutting equipment, consisting of a rotary cutter used with an acrylic ruler and self-healing cutting mat, has speeded up the process of cutting shapes and made it more accurate; the sewing machine makes assembling the patchwork and quilting the finished piece quick and easy.

SEWING MACHINES

Ever more sophisticated, computerized machines are now available, but even a machine with just a straight stitch will speed up the process of assembling and quilting the patchwork considerably. Most sewing machines have a swing needle that allows the zigzag stitching used for securing appliqué patches. Machines with decorative stitches provide the opportunity for additional embellishments.

LONGARM QUILTING MACHINES

These machines are used by professional quilters. You can choose from a huge library of quilting designs. There is also the option to have edge-to-edge quilting, quilting of one design over the entire quilt, or a combination of patterns to complement each other. Alternatively, you can specify your own freehand style.

One of the advantages of this machine is that the quilt sandwich does not need to be tacked or pinned together prior to quilting: the pieced top, batting and backing are mounted onto separate rollers that are part of the frame of the machine.

The machine is hand operated and takes considerable skill to work successfully. Most of the quilters who offer this quilting service advertise in patchwork magazines.

ROTARY CUTTING

Rotary cutting has become the most commonly used method of cutting fabrics for patchwork. Most rotary cutting tools are available with either imperial or metric measurements.

Rotary Cutters

There are several different types available, mainly in three different sizes: small, medium and large. The medium size is probably the one most widely used and perhaps the easiest to control. The smallest can be difficult to use with rulers. The largest is very useful when cutting through several layers of fabric but can take some practice to use. The rotary blade is extremely sharp, so be sure to observe the safety instructions. It does become blunted with frequent use, so it is always worth having a spare.

Rotary Rulers

Various different rulers are available for use with rotary cutters. These are

---

SAFETY

All rotary cutters have some form of safety mechanism that should always be used. Close the safety cover over the blade after every cut you make, whether or not you intend to continue with another cut. Safety habits are essential and will help prevent accidents. Ensure that the cutters are safely stored out of the reach of children.

Keep the cutter clean and free of lint. An occasional drop of sewing machine oil helps it to rotate smoothly. Avoid running over pins, as this ruins the blade. Renew the blade as soon as it becomes blunt, as a blunt blade makes for inaccurate and difficult cutting and can damage the cutting mat. Replacement blades are readily available and there are also blade sharpening/exchange services.

made of acrylic and are sufficiently thick to act as a guide for the rotary blade. You must use these rulers with the rotary cutter. Do not use metal rulers, as they will severely damage the blades.

The rulers are marked with measurements and angled lines to use as a guide when cutting the fabrics. Ideally, these markings should be on the underside of the ruler, laser printed and easy to read. Angles should be marked in both directions. Different makes of rulers can have the lines printed in different colors. Choose one that you find easy on your eyes. Some makes also have a non-slip surface on the back, which is helpful.

The two most useful rulers are either a 24 x 6 in/60 x 15 cm, or one that is slightly shorter, and the small bias square ruler, 6½ in or 15 cm.

NOTES

Seams

Unless otherwise stated, the seam allowances are included in the measurements given and are always ¼ in for imperial and 0.75 cm for metric. The metric seam allowance is slightly bigger than the imperial, but it is easy to use in conjunction with the various rotary cutting rulers on the market.

Measurements

The measurements in the quilt instructions are given in both imperial and metric. Use only one set of measurements in any project – do not interchange them, because they are not direct equivalents.

This ruler is particularly useful for marking squares containing two triangles – the half-square triangle units. There are many other rulers designed for specific jobs that you can purchase if and when needed.

Self-Healing Rotary Cutting Mats
These are essential companions to the rotary cutter and ruler. Do not attempt to cut on any other surface. The mats come in a range of sizes and several different colors. The smaller ones are useful to take to classes, but for use at home, purchase the largest that you can afford and that suits your own workstation. There is usually a grid on one side, although both sides can be used. The lines on the mat are not always accurate, so it's better to use the lines on the ruler if possible.

OTHER USEFUL EQUIPMENT

Most other pieces of equipment are those that you will already have in your sewing kit. Those listed below are essential, but there is also a vast array of special tools devised by experienced quiltmakers that have specific uses. They are not needed by the beginner quilter but can really enhance the planning, cutting and quilting of your designs.

Scissors: Two pairs are needed. One large pair of good-quality scissors should be used exclusively for cutting fabric. The second, smaller pair is for cutting paper, card or template plastic.

Markers: Quilting designs can either be traced or drawn on the fabric prior to the layering or added after the layering with the aid of stencils or templates. Various marking tools are available: 2H pencils; silver,

yellow or white pencils; fade-away or washable marking pens; and Hera markers (which lightly indent the fabric). Whatever your choice, test the markers on a scrap of the fabric used in the quilt to ensure that the marks can be removed.

Pins: Good-quality, clean, rustproof, straight pins are essential when a pin is required to hold the work in place for piecing. Flat-headed flower pins are useful because they don't add bulk.

Safety pins: Special quilters' safety pins with curved sides are useful for holding the quilt "sandwich" together for quilting, especially for those who prefer to machine quilt or want the speed of not tacking/basting the three layers together.

Needles: For hand quilting, use "quilting" or "betweens" needles. Most quilters start with a no. 8 or 9 and progress to a no. 10 or 12. For machine stitching, the needles numbered 70/10 or 80/12 are both suitable for piecing and quilting. For making ties with thicker thread, use a crewel or embroidery needle.

Thimbles: Two thimbles will be required for hand quilting. One thimble is worn on the hand pushing the needle and the other on the hand underneath the quilt "receiving" the needle. There are various types on the market ranging from metal to plastic to leather sheaths for the finger. There are also little patches that stick to the finger to protect it.

HOOPS AND FRAMES

These are only needed if you are quilting by hand. They hold a section of the quilt under light tension to help you to achieve an even stitch. There are many types and sizes available, ranging from round and oval hoops to standing frames made of plastic pipes, and wooden fixed frames.

Hoops are perhaps the easiest for a beginner. The 14 in/35 cm or 16 in/ 40 cm are best for portability. When the quilt is in the hoop, the surface of the quilt should not be taut, as is the case with embroidery. If you place the quilt top with its hoop on a table, you should be able to push the fabric in the center of the hoop with your finger and touch the table beneath. Without this "give," you will not be able to "rock" the needle for the quilting stitch. Do not leave the quilt in a hoop when you are not working on it, as the hoop will distort the fabrics.

TECHNIQUES

ROTARY CUTTING

The basis of rotary cutting is that fabric is cut first in strips – usually across the width of the fabric – then cross-cut into squares or rectangles. Unless otherwise stated, fabric is used folded selvage to selvage, wrong sides together, as it has come off the bolt.

MAKING THE EDGE STRAIGHT

Before any accurate cutting can be done, you must first make sure the cut edge of the fabric is at right angles to the selvages.

1 Place the folded fabric on the cutting mat with the fabric smoothed out, the selvages exactly aligned at the top and the bulk of the fabric on the side that is not your cutting hand. Place the ruler on the fabric next to the cut edge, aligning the horizontal lines on the ruler with the fold and with the selvages.

2 Place your non-cutting hand on the ruler to hold it straight and apply pressure. Keep the hand holding the ruler in line with the cutting hand. Place the cutter on the mat just below the fabric and up against the ruler. Start cutting by running the cutter upwards and right next to the edge of the ruler (diagram 1).

diagram 1

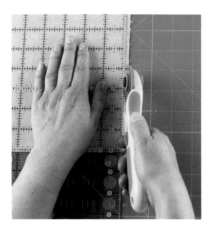

3 When the cutter becomes level with your extended fingertips, stop cutting but leave the cutter in position and carefully move the hand holding the ruler further along the ruler to keep the applied pressure in the area where the cutting is taking place. Continue cutting and moving the steadying hand as necessary until you have cut completely across the fabric. As soon as the cut is complete, close the safety shield on the cutter. If you run out of cutting mat, you will need to reposition the fabric, but this is not ideal as it can bring the fabric out of alignment.

4 Open out the narrow strip of fabric just cut off. Check to make sure that a "valley" or a "hill" has not appeared at the point of the fold on the edge just cut; it should be perfectly straight. If it is not, the

fabric was not folded correctly. Fold the fabric again, making sure that this time the selvages are exactly aligned. Make another cut to straighten the edge and check again.

CUTTING STRIPS

The next stage is to cut strips across the width of the fabric. To do this, change the position of the fabric to the opposite side of the board, then use the measurements on the ruler to cut the strips, as follows:

1 Place the fabric on the cutting mat on the side of your cutting hand. Place the ruler on the mat so that it overlaps the fabric. Align the cut edge of the fabric with the vertical line on the ruler that corresponds to the measurement that you wish to cut. The horizontal lines on the ruler should be aligned with the folded edge and the selvage of the fabric.

2 As before, place one hand on the ruler to apply pressure while cutting the fabric with the other hand (diagram 2).

diagram 2

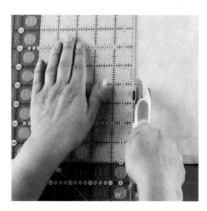

CROSS-CUTTING

The strips can now be cut into smaller units, described as cross-cutting, and these units are sometimes sub-cut into triangles.

Squares

1 Place the strip just cut on the cutting mat with the longest edge horizontal to you and most of the fabric on the side of the non-cutting hand. Cut off the selvages in the same way in which you straightened the fabric edge at the start of the process.

2 Now place the strip on the opposite side of the mat and cut across (cross-cut) the strip using the same measurement on the ruler as used for cutting the strip; ensure that the horizontal lines of the ruler align with the horizontal edges of the fabric. You have now created two squares of the required measurement (diagram 3). Repeat as required.

diagram 3

Rectangles

1 First cut a strip to one of the required side measurements for the rectangle. Remove the selvages.

2 Turn the strip to the horizontal position as for the squares.

3 Cross-cut this strip using the other side measurement required for the rectangle. Again, ensure that the horizontal lines of the ruler align with the horizontal cut edges of the strip.

Multi-Strip Units

This two-stage method of cutting strips, then cross-cutting into squares or rectangles, can also be used to speed up the cutting of multi-strip units to provide strip blocks, such as used for the Tumbling Blocks on page 72.

1 Cut the required number and size of strips and stitch together as per the instructions for the block/quilt you are making. Press the seams and check that they are smooth on the right side of the strip unit with no pleats or wrinkles.

2 Place the unit right side up in the horizontal position on the cutting mat. Align the horizontal lines on the ruler with the longer cut edges of the strips and with the seam lines just created (diagram 4). If, after you have cut a few cross-cuts, the lines on the ruler do not line up with the cut edges as well as the seam lines, re-cut the end to straighten it before cutting any more units.

diagram 4

ROTARY CUTTING TRIANGLES

Squares can be divided into either two or four triangles, called half-square or quarter-square triangles. Both sizes of triangle can be quickly cut using the rotary cutter or they

can be made even faster by a quick piecing method described on pages 11 and 12.

Cutting Half-Square Triangles

1 Cut the fabric into strips of the correct depth and remove the selvages.

2 Cross-cut the strips into squares of the correct width.

3 Align the 45° angle line on the ruler with the sides of the square and place the edge of the ruler so that it goes diagonally across the square from corner to corner. Cut the square on this diagonal, creating two half-square triangles.

Cutting Quarter-Square Triangles

1 Cut the fabric into strips of the correct depth and remove the selvages.

2 Cross-cut the strips into squares of the correct width.

3 Cut the square into two half-square triangles, as above.

4 You can either repeat this procedure on the other diagonal or, if you are wary of the fabric slipping now that it is in two pieces, separate the two triangles and cut them individually. Align one of the horizontal lines of the ruler with the long edge of the triangle, the 45° line with the short edge of the triangle and the edge of the ruler placed on the point of the triangle opposite the long edge. Cut this half-square triangle into two quarter-square triangles.

SEAMS

To stitch accurately, you must be able to use the correct seam allowance without having to mark it on the fabric. To do this, you use either the foot or the bed of your sewing machine as a guide. Many machines have a "¼ in" or "patchwork" foot available as an extra. Before you start any piecing, check that you can stitch this seam allowance accurately.

Checking the Machine for the Correct Seam Allowance

Unthread the machine. Place a piece of paper under the presser foot, so that the right-hand edge of the paper aligns with the right-hand edge of the presser foot. Stitch a seam line on the paper. A row of holes will appear. Remove the paper from the machine and measure the distance from the holes to the edge of the paper. If it is not the correct width, i.e. ¼ in/ 0.75 cm, try one of the following:

1 If your machine has a number of different needle positions, try moving the needle in the direction required to make the seam allowance accurate. Try the test of stitching a row of holes again.

2 Draw a line on the paper to the correct seam allowance, i.e. ¼ in/ 0.75 cm from the edge of the paper. Place the paper under the presser foot, aligning the drawn line with the needle. Lower the presser foot to hold the paper securely and, to double-check, lower the needle to ensure that it is directly on top of the drawn line.

Fix a piece of masking tape on the bed of the machine so that the left-hand edge of the tape lines up with the right-hand edge of the paper. This can also be done with magnetic strips available on the market to be used as seam guides. But do take advice on using these if your machine is computerized or electronic.

Stitching ¼ in/0.75 cm Seams

When stitching pieces together, line up the edge of the fabric with the right-hand edge of the presser foot, or with the left-hand edge of the tape or the magnetic strip on the bed of your machine, depending on which method you have used.

Checking the Fabric for the Correct Seam Allowance

As so much of the success of a patchwork depends on accuracy of cutting and seaming, it is worth double-checking on the fabric that you are in fact stitching a ¼ in/0.75 cm seam.

Cut three strips of fabric 1½ in/ 4 cm wide. Stitch these together along the long edges to make a multi-strip unit of three pieces. Press the seams away from the center strip. Measure the center strip. It should measure exactly 1 in/2.5 cm wide. If not, reposition the needle/tape and try again.

Stitch Length

The stitch length used is normally 12 stitches to the inch or 5 to the centimeter. If the pieces being stitched together are to be cross-cut into smaller units, it is advisable to slightly shorten the stitch, which will mean the seam is less likely to unravel. It is also good practice to start each new project with a new needle in a clean machine – free of lint around the bobbin housing.

QUICK MACHINE PIECING

The three most basic techniques are for stitching pairs of patches together (chain piecing), for stitching half-square triangle units and for stitching quarter-square triangle units.

Chain Piecing

Have all the pairs of patches or strips together ready in a pile. Place the first two patches or strips in the machine, right sides together, and stitch them together. Just before reaching the end, stop stitching and pick up the next two patches or strips. Place them on the bed of the machine, so that they just touch the patches under the needle. Stitch off one set and onto the next. Repeat this process until all the pairs are stitched to create a "chain" of pieced patches/strips (diagram 5). Cut the thread between each unit to separate them. Open out and press the seams according to the instructions given with each project.

diagram 5

Stitching Half-Square Triangle Units

This is a quick method of creating a bi-colored square without cutting the triangles first.

1 Cut two squares of different colored fabrics to the correct measurement, i.e. the finished size of the bi-colored square plus ⅝ in /1.75 cm. Place them right sides together, aligning all raw edges. On the wrong side of the top square, draw a diagonal line from one corner to the other (diagram 6).

diagram 6

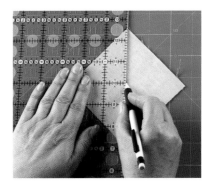

2 Stitch ¼ in/0.75 cm away on either side of the drawn line, chain piecing the units to save time (diagram 7).

diagram 7

3 Cut along the drawn line to separate the two halves. Open out and press the seams according to the instructions given with each project. You now have two squares, each containing two triangles (diagram 8). Trim off the corners.

diagram 8

PRESSING

Each project will have instructions on the direction in which to press the seam allowances. These have been designed to facilitate piecing at junctions and to reduce the bulk so that seam allowances do not lie one on top of the other. Pressing as you complete each stage of the piecing will also improve the accuracy and look of your work. Take care not to distort the patches. Be gentle, not fierce, with the iron.

ADDING THE BORDERS

Most patchwork tops are framed by one or more borders. The simplest way of adding borders is to add strips first to the top and bottom of the quilt and then to the sides, producing abutted corners. A more complicated method is to add strips to adjacent sides and join them with seams at 45 degrees, giving mitered borders. Only the first method is used for the quilts in this book.

Adding Borders with Abutted Corners

The measurements for the borders required for each quilt in the book will be given in the instructions. However, it is always wise to measure your own work to determine the actual measurement.

1 Measure the quilt through the center across the width edge to edge. Cut the strips for the top and bottom borders to this length by the width specified for the border.

2 Pin the strips to the quilt by pinning first at each end, then in the middle, then evenly spaced along the edge. By pinning in this manner, it is possible to ensure that the quilt "fits" the border (diagram

diagram 9

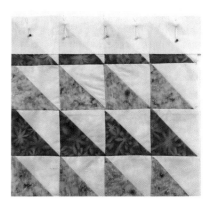

9). Stitch the border strips into position on the top and bottom edge of the quilt. Press the seams towards the border.

3 Measure the quilt through the center from top to bottom. Cut the side border strips to this measurement.

4 Pin and stitch the borders to each side of the quilt as before (diagram 10). Press the seams towards the border.

diagram 10

APPLIQUÉ

Applied motifs can be stitched either by hand or by machine and there are different methods for each type.

Needle turn appliqué

This is a hand stitching method. It involves two layers, the top layer being the appliqué fabric. This is cut with a seam allowance which is then turned under. Two different methods are used in the book, one using freezer paper as the underneath material and the other ordinary paper.

Freezer Paper Method

Freezer paper, originally marketed as a paper to wrap frozen goods, has been appropriated by quilters to use in appliqué work because it lightly adheres to fabric but can be lifted and repositioned without damaging it. Freezer paper can be obtained from quilting suppliers.

1 To practice this method, draw a simple shape, such as a leaf. Place a piece of freezer paper, shiny side down, over the shape, and trace on to the matte side. It's important to work on the matte side as the shiny side provides the sticky surface which will adhere to the fabric.

2 Cut the leaf motif from the freezer paper shape exactly on the marked line. Place shiny side down on the reverse of the appliqué fabric, which needs to be slightly bigger than the motif to allow for a seam, and iron to hold in position. Trim the fabric to the shape of the leaf motif but allowing a seam allowance of a scant ¼ in/0.75 cm all around.

3 Pin the leaf (with freezer paper still in place) to the background fabric using appliqué pins. Using thread to match the appliqué shape, thread a needle, then bring the needle to the front of the fabric. Use the tip of the needle to turn under the seam allowance on the leaf shape. You will be able to feel the freezer paper inside, and you can use it as an edge against which you can turn the fabric, creating a crisp fold. Take a

tiny appliqué stitch (like a slip-stitch) on the fold of the material, from the front to the back of the work to stitch down this fold.

Continue in the same way around the leaf until you are about 1 in/2.5 cm from the beginning. At this point, you can remove the freezer paper. Finish slip-stitching the motif.

Paper Template

This is an alternative hand-stitched method.

1 Make a paper template of a simple shape, such as a leaf, then use it to cut out the fabric appliqué shape with ¼ in/0.75 cm seam allowance as in step 2 above. Place the paper template on the reverse of the fabric and pin in the middle to hold in place. Fold over the seam allowance and loosely baste in place, then remove the pin.

2 Pin this piece to the background fabric and stitch using a tiny appliqué stitch as before. The paper can either be left in place permanently or can be removed through a tiny incision from the reverse side in the background fabric. Remove the basting stitches.

Bonded Appliqué

This is a faster method, which is usually machine-stitched. In this case the backing to the fabric is cut from fusible webbing. The fabric is cut to the exact shape of the motif, so no seam allowances are involved, making it especially suitable for small, intricate shapes. Fusible webbing is very thin fabric glue, attached to a sheet of transparent paper. Initially it will be rough on one side (the glue side) and smooth on the other.

1 Either draw your chosen shape directly on to the smooth side of the fusible webbing or, if you are making a number of copies of the same shape, make a template of the shape from lightweight card stock or paper, then trace on to the smooth side of the fusible webbing. Cut out roughly outside the marked line.

2 Place the fabric for the appliqué wrong side up on the work surface and put the fusible webbing shape, rough side down, on top. Iron to fix in place. Now cut the shape out exactly on the marked line.

3 Peel off the paper backing, then position the shape in the appropriate position on the background fabric, glue side down. carefully iron it to bond the two fabrics together.

4 Machine-stitch in place with a satin or zigzag stitch. The ideal is to just cover the edge of the shape, without stitching too much into the background fabric. Alternatively, you could stitch the motif down by hand using a close blanket stitch.

NOTE

When the motif is traced on to the backing paper, it will be reversed when you finally iron it in place. If you want a true image, i.e. the same way around, you must trace the image on tracing paper, reverse it and trace again on to the fusible web.

QUILTING

The three layers or "sandwich" of the backing/batting/pieced top that make up a patchwork quilt are held together by quilting or by tying. The quilting can be done by hand or machine. The tying is done by hand-stitching decorative ties at strategic points on the quilt, which adds to the overall effect.

Layering/Sandwiching

Prior to any quilting, unless you are using a longarm quilting machine (see page 7), the pieced top must be layered with the batting and the backing. The batting and the backing should be slightly larger than the quilt top – approximately 2 in/5 cm on all sides. There are two different methods for assembling the three layers, depending on whether the quilt has bound edges or not.

Assembling Prior to Binding

1 Lay out the backing fabric wrong side uppermost. Ensure that it is stretched out and smooth. Secure the edges with masking tape at intervals along the edges to help hold it in position.

2 Place the batting on top of the backing fabric. If you need to join two pieces of batting first, butt the edges and stitch together by hand using a herringbone stitch (diagram 11).

3 Place the pieced top right side up and centered on top of the batting.

Basting Prior to Quilting

If the piece is to be quilted rather than tied, the three layers now need to be held together at regular intervals. This can be done by basting or by using safety pins. For either

diagram 11

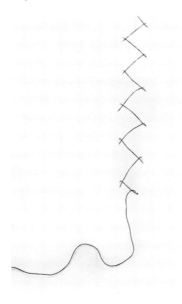

method, start in the center of the quilt and work out to the edges.

To baste the layers together, using a long length of thread, start basting in the center of the quilt top. Pull about half of the thread through as you start stitching. When you reach the edge, go back and baste the other end of the thread to the opposite edge. Repeat this process, stitching in a grid of horizontal and vertical lines all over the quilt top (diagram 12).

diagram 12

If using safety pins, place the pins at regular intervals all over the quilt surface (diagram 13).

diagram 13

MACHINE QUILTING

Designs to be used for machine quilting should ideally be those that have one continuous line. The lines can be straight or free-form curves and squiggles. For either type, be sure to keep the density of stitching the same. With either method, continuous lines of stitching will be visible both on the top and on the back of the quilt. It is a quick method but requires careful preparation.

There is a wide variety of tools available designed to help make handling the quilt easier during the machine quilting process. Some machines require a walking foot to stitch the three layers together. These are used with the feed dogs up and, while in use, the machine controls the direction and stitch length. However, the most essential requirement is practice.

It is worth making up a practice sandwich – if possible using the same fabrics and batting as used in the actual quilt – to be sure that you get the effect you want. In any case, plan the quilting design first, otherwise there is a danger that you will start with quite dense stitching, then tire of the process and begin to space out the lines, producing an uneven pattern.

When starting and stopping the stitching during machine quilting, either reduce the stitch length to zero or stitch several stitches in one spot. If you do not like the build-up of stitches that this method produces, leave long tails on the thread when you start and stop. Later, pull these threads through to one side of the quilt, knot them, then thread them into a needle. Push the needle into the fabric and into the batting, but not through to the other side of the quilt, and then back out through the fabric again about 1 in/2.5 cm away from where the needle entered the quilt. Cut off the excess thread.

In-the-Ditch Machine Quilting

One of the easiest and most common forms of straight line quilting is called "in-the-ditch" and involves stitching along a seam line where it is almost invisible (diagram 14). To do this, slightly part the fabric at the seam, then let it settle back after stitching.

diagram 14

Echo Quilting

This is also a popular type of straight line quilting where the quilting is stitched ¼ in/0.75 cm away from the shape or seam line (diagram 15).

diagram 15

Free Motion Machine Quilting

When machine quilting in freehand, a darning foot is used with the feed dogs down, so that you can move the quilt in all directions. This is easier on some machines than others, but all require some practice. The design shown here is called vermicelli (diagram 16).

diagram 16

HAND QUILTING

Place the section of the quilt to be worked on in a hoop as described on page 8. The stitch used for hand quilting is a running stitch. The needle goes into the quilt through to the back and returns to the top of the quilt all in one movement. The aim is to have the size of the stitches and spaces between them the same length.

1 Thread a needle with an 18 in/ 45 cm length of quilting thread and knot the end. Push the needle into the fabric and into the batting, but not through to the back, about 1 in/2.5 cm away from where you want to start stitching. Bring the needle up through the fabric at the point where you will begin stitching. Gently pull on the thread to "pop" the knot through into the batting.

2 To make a perfect quilting stitch, the needle needs to enter the fabric perpendicular to the quilt top. Holding the needle between your first finger and thumb, push the needle into the fabric until it hits the thimble on the finger of the hand underneath.

3 The needle can now be held between the thimble on your sewing hand and the thimble on the finger underneath. Release your thumb and first finger hold on the needle. Place your thumb on the quilt top just in front of where the needle will come back up to the top and gently press down on the quilt (diagram 17).

diagram 17

4 At the same time, rock the thread end of the needle down towards the quilt top and push the needle up from underneath so that

the point appears on the top of the quilt. You can either pull the needle through now, making only one stitch, or rock the needle up to the vertical again, push the needle through to the back, then rock the needle up to the quilt top, again placing another stitch on the needle. Repeat until you can no longer rock the needle into a completely upright position (diagram 18). Pull the needle through the quilt. One stitch at a time, or several placed on the needle at once – "the rocking stitch" – before pulling the thread through, are both acceptable.

diagram 18

5 When the stitching is complete, tie a knot in the thread close to the quilt surface. Push the needle into the quilt top and the batting next to the knot, but not through to the back of the quilt. Bring the needle up again about 1 in/2.5 cm away and gently tug on the thread to "pop" the knot through the fabric and into the batting. Cut the thread close to the surface.

BINDING

Once the quilting is completed, the quilt is usually (but not always) finished off with a binding to enclose the raw edges. This binding can be cut on the straight or on the bias. Either way, the binding is usually best done with a double fold. It can be applied in four separate pieces to each of the four sides, or the binding strips can be joined together and stitched to the quilt in one continuous strip with mitered corners. To join straight-cut pieces for a continuous strip, use straight seams; to join bias-cut pieces, use diagonal seams (diagram 19).

diagram 19

For either method, the width of the bias strips should be cut to the following measurement: finished binding width x four + the seam allowance x two.

For example:
A finished binding width of ½ in would be cut as 2½ in:
(½ in x 4) + (¼ in x 2) = 2½ in
or 1.25 cm would be cut 6.5 cm:
(1.25 cm x 4) + (0.75 cm x 2) = 6.5 cm

Continuous Strip Binding

1 Fold the binding in half lengthwise with wrong sides together and lightly press.

2 Place the raw edges of the binding to the raw edge of the quilt – somewhere along one side, not at a corner. Commence stitching about 1 in/2.5 cm from the end of the binding and, using the specified seam allowance, stitch the binding to the quilt through all layers of the "sandwich" (diagram 20). Stop ¼ in/0.75 cm from the end. At this point, backstitch to secure, then break off the threads. Remove the quilt from the sewing machine.

3 Place the quilt on a flat surface, with the binding just stitched at the top edge; fold the binding up and away from the quilt to "twelve o'clock," creating a 45° fold at the corner (diagram 20).

diagram 20

4 Fold the binding back down to "six o'clock," aligning the raw edges of the binding to the raw edge of the quilt. The fold created on the binding at the top should be the same distance away from the seam as the width of the finished binding (diagram 21).

diagram 21

5 Start stitching the binding to the quilt at the same point where the previous stitching stopped. Secure with backstitching, then continue to the next corner. Repeat the process at each corner.

6 Stop about 2 in/5 cm from where you started. Open out the fold on both ends of the binding, then seam the two ends together. Trim away the excess, refold and finish applying the binding to the quilt.

7 Trim the excess batting and backing fabric so that the distance from the stitching line equals or is slightly wider than that of the finished binding. Fold the binding over to the back and hand stitch the folded edge of the binding to the quilt along the row of machine stitching just created (diagram 22). A miter will appear at the corners on the front and on the back of the binding. Slip-stitch these in place.

diagram 22

Binding the Four Sides Separately

1 Cut binding strips to the required width. Fold in half lengthwise with wrong sides together and lightly press.

2 Measure the pieced top through the center from top to bottom and cut two of the binding strips to this length.

3 Pin one of the strips down the side of the quilt, right sides together and aligning raw edges. Stitch with the usual seam allowance. Trim the excess batting and backing fabric so that the distance from the stitching line equals or is slightly wider than that of the finished binding (diagram 23).

diagram 23

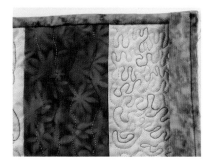

4 Fold the binding strip to the back of the quilt and slip-stitch to the backing fabric. Trim the ends level with the batting. Do the same on the opposite side of the quilt with the other strip.

5 Measure the quilt through the center from side to side and add 1½ in/4 cm for turnings. Cut two more binding strips to this length, joining if necessary. Stitch to the top and bottom of the quilt, leaving a ¾ in/2 cm overhang at each end. Trim the backing and batting as above. Then turn in a short hem at either end before folding to the back and slip-stitching down. Slip-stitch the corners neatly.

HANGING SLEEVE

If your quilt is a wallhanging or is to be exhibited, it will need a hanging sleeve. A sleeve can be added after the quilt is completely finished, but a more secure and permanent sleeve can be added along with the binding.

1 Cut a piece of fabric, preferably matching the backing, to measure 10 in/25 cm deep by the width of the quilt. Make a 1 in/ 2.5 cm hem on both the short ends.

2 Fold the fabric in half along the length with wrong sides together. Center this on the back of the quilt, aligning the raw edges of the sleeve with the raw edges of the quilt. Pin, then tack.

3 Turn the quilt over so the front is uppermost. Stitch the binding in the normal way, which will then secure the hanging sleeve at the same time (diagram 24).

diagram 24

4 Finish hand stitching on the binding.

5 Lay the quilt on a flat surface with the back uppermost. Smooth out the sleeve and pin the lower edge so that it rests evenly on the back of the quilt.

6 Stitch the sleeve to the back of the quilt along the fold at the bottom of the sleeve, then stitch the underneath edge at each short end, so that when a rod is inserted it will not actually touch the back of the quilt, only the sleeve fabric. Take care that your stitches only go into the back and batting of the quilt and are not visible on the front. Remove the pins.

1. JACOB'S LADDER

Designed by Jane Coombes

JACOB'S LADDER IS THE NAME of the traditional patchwork block that forms the basis for the central part of this lap quilt or throw. The design features geometric lines accentuated by the use of fabrics in strong contrasting colors. It also works well when similar shades of one color are used for a blended look. The pieced border is also traditional and is called "sawtooth."

JACOB'S LADDER

Quilt Plan

FINISHED SIZE: 45 ⅞ X 63 ⅞ IN/112 X 154 CM

MATERIALS

All fabrics used in the quilt are 42–44 in/107–115 cm wide, 100% cotton.

Triangles: white, 3/4 yard/70 cm

Squares: gray, 3/4 yard/70 cm

Triangles, border and binding:
black, 1 3/4 yards/1.7 m

Squares and border pieces:
red, 1 1/4 yards/1.2 m

Backing: 2 3/4 yards/2.5 m

Batting: 50 x 70 in/125 x 167 cm

Thread: 100% cotton for piecing;
invisible thread, black/gray and
black/red twisted rayon machine
embroidery threads for machine
quilting

ALTERNATIVE COLOR SCHEMES

1 Gently contrasting pastels for a soft, romantic look.

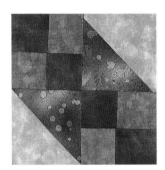

2 Similar shades of one color for a blended look.

*3 Black, gray and white for a strong,
masculine look.*

*4 A dominant color for the diagonal small squares for a
different design emphasis.*

CUTTING

1 From the white fabric, cut five strips, $3^7/8$ in/9.5 cm deep, across the width of the fabric. Cross-cut these to produce forty-eight $3^7/8$ in/9.5 cm squares.

2 From the gray fabric, cut 12 strips, 2 in/5 cm deep, across the width of the fabric.

3 From the black fabric, cut the following pieces:
   • five strips, $3^7/8$ in/9.5 cm deep, across the width of the fabric. Cross-cut these to produce forty-eight $3^7/8$ in/9.5 cm squares.
   • five strips, 2 in/5.5 cm deep, across the width of the fabric, for Border 1.
   • four strips, 4 in/12.5 cm deep, across the width of the fabric. Cross-cut these into 17 rectangles measuring $2^7/8$ x 4 in/7 x 12.5 cm, 23 rectangles measuring $3^1/8$ x 4 in/7.75 x 12.5 cm and one $16^1/2$ x 2 in/50 x 6 cm strip, for Border 2.
   • six strips, $2^1/4$ in/5.5 cm deep, across the width of the fabric, for the binding.

4 From the red fabric, cut the following pieces:
   • twelve strips, 2 in/5 cm deep, across the width of the fabric.
   • four strips, 4 in/12.5 cm deep, across the width of the fabric. Cross-cut these into 17 rectangles measuring $2^7/8$ x 4 in/7 x 12.5 cm, 23 rectangles measuring $3^1/8$ x 4 in/7.75 x 12.5 cm, one $16^1/2$ x 2 in/50 x 6 cm strip, four $1^5/8$ x $3^1/2$ in/4 x 10.5 cm rectangles and four $1^3/4$ x $3^1/2$ in/4.25 x 10.5 cm rectangles, for Border 2.

5 Cut the backing fabric across the width of the fabric into two equal lengths.

STITCHING

1 Start by making the black and white half-square triangles (see also pages 11 and 12, diagrams 6–7). Draw a diagonal line across the wrong side of a white $3^7/8$ in/9.5 cm square. Place against a black square of the same size, right sides together. Pin then stitch $1/4$ in/ 0.75 cm either side of the line. Press as stitched to embed the stitches and to avoid stretching, then carefully cut along the penciled line (*diagram 1*) and press the seam

allowances towards the dark fabric. Repeat the process to make a total of 96 black and white half-square triangles.

diagram 1

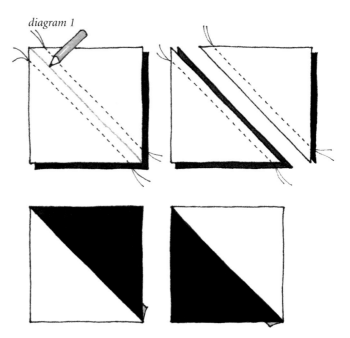

2 Now make the gray and red patchwork square units. With right sides together and taking a $1/4$ in/0.75 cm seam allowance, pin then stitch together the longest edges of the gray and red 2 in/5 cm strips. Press the seam allowances towards the darkest fabric then cross-cut into 240 units, 2 in/5 cm wide (*diagram 2*).

3 Taking the usual seam allowance, join these two-square gray and red units together in pairs (*diagram 2*) to make 120 four-square units. Press the seam allowances to one side.

diagram 2

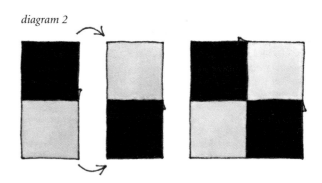

4 Referring to *diagram 3*, join the black and white half-square triangles with the gray and red units. Stitch three units together into a row first, then join the rows to complete 12 blocks of nine units. Note: press the seam

allowances from Rows 1 and 3 in the same direction, and press the seam allowances from Row 2 in the opposite direction. This allows the seam allowances to "butt up" to aid accurate matching of seams.

diagram 3

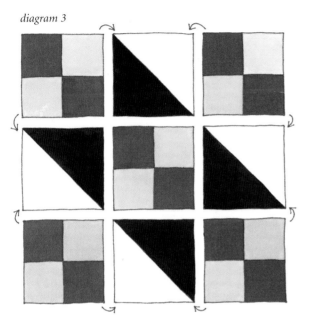

5 Repeat Step 4, referring this time to *diagram 4*, to make another 12 blocks of nine units.

diagram 4

6 Lay out the 24 "Jacob's Ladder" blocks for the center of the quilt, according to the quilt plan on page 20. Taking the usual seam allowance, pin then stitch the blocks into rows and press the seam allowances to one side. As before, press the seam allowances of Row 1 to the left, Row 2 to the right, Row 3 to the left, and so on.

7 Join the rows to complete the joining of the blocks for this section. Press the seam allowances towards the bottom of the quilt.

ADDING THE BORDERS

1 To make Border 1, cut two of the black Border 1 strips to a length of $36^1/2$ in/85.5 cm. Taking the usual seam allowance, pin and stitch the strips to the top and bottom edges of the quilt. Press the seam allowances towards these strips.

2 Join the remaining three black Border 1 strips with diagonal seams to make a continuous length. Press the seam allowances open. (For sewing diagonal seams, see page 16, diagram 22.)

3 Cut this strip into two lengths of $57^1/2$ in/135.5 cm and pin and stitch to the side edges of the quilt. Press.

4 To make Border 2, lay the red and black $2^7/8$ x 4 in/ 7 x 12.5 cm rectangles right side uppermost, then cut them diagonally in half from top left to bottom right. Note: direction is very important.

5 Place the rotary ruler over each triangle and trim off the excess points at either end of the diagonal side (*diagram 5*). This will aid in accurate piecing of these triangles.

diagram 5

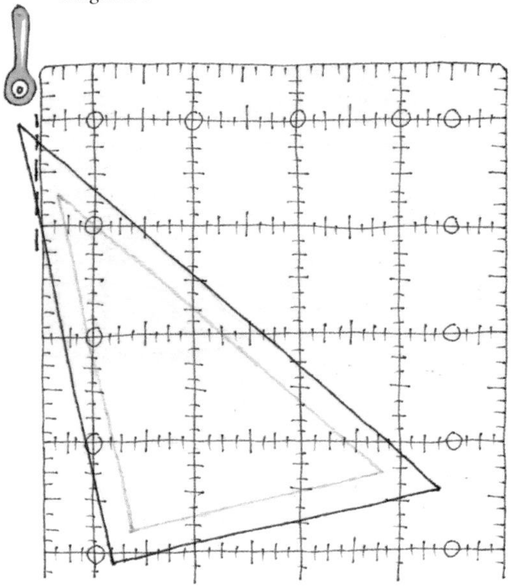

6 Pin and stitch the red and black triangles together in pairs along the diagonal edges (*diagram 6*) to make 34 stitched rectangles. Press the seam allowances towards the red triangles.

diagram 6

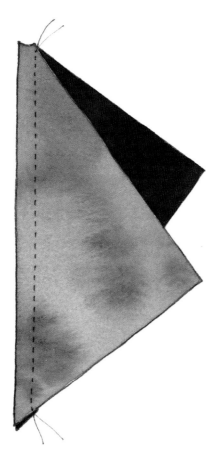

8 Pin and stitch one red $1^5/_8$ x $3^1/_2$ in/4 x 10.5 cm filler strip to each end of these rows. Press the seam allowances towards these strips.

9 Taking the usual seam allowance, join these sawtooth border strips to the top and bottom edges of the quilt. Press the seam allowances towards Border 1.

10 Make 46 more stitched rectangles by repeating Steps 4–6 and using the red and black $3^1/_8$ x 4 in/7.75 x 12.5 cm rectangles. Trim off the points as before to aid accurate piecing.

11 Join these stitched rectangles into two rows of 23 blocks each. Stitch one red $1^3/_4$ x $3^1/_2$ in/4.25 x 10.5 cm filler strip to each end of these rows. Press the seam allowances towards these strips.

12 Make the red and black four-patch corner blocks in the same way as the gray and red patchwork blocks in Steps 2 and 3 of "Stitching." Strip-piece together the longest edges of the black and red $16^1/_2$ x 2 in/50 x 6 cm strips. Cross-cut into eight 2 in/6 cm units (*diagram 2*), then join these in pairs (*diagram 3*) to make four four-square blocks and press the seam allowances to one side.

13 Referring to the quilt plan on page 20, stitch one of these four-patch blocks to each end of the border strips constructed in Step 11. Press the seam allowances towards the filler strips.

14 Taking the usual seam allowance, join these sawtooth border strips to the side edges of the quilt. Press the seam allowances towards Border 1.

7 Join the stitched rectangles constructed in Step 6 into two rows of 17 blocks each (*diagram 7*). Press the seam allowances towards the black triangles.

diagram 7

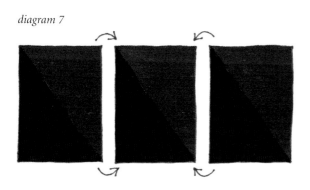

FINISHING

1 Press the backing fabric, remove the selvages and join the two lengths of fabric together along one of the edges that has just been trimmed. Use a $1/2$ in/1.5 cm seam allowance and press the seam open.

2 Spread the backing right side down on a flat surface, then smooth out the batting and the patchwork top, right side up, on top, positioning it so that there is an equal amount of surplus batting and backing fabric on all four sides. Fasten together with safety pins or baste in a grid.

3 Machine quilt in-the-ditch around the blocks using invisible thread. (For In-the-Ditch Machine Quilting instructions, see page 15 and diagram 17.)

4 Add further lines of straight machine quilting to emphasize the diagonal zigzag pattern of the "Jacob's ladder" blocks, using a black/gray twisted rayon machine embroidery thread on the spool and 100% cotton thread on the bobbin. Apply free motion machine quilting using invisible thread between the zigzag patterning. Quilt Border 1 using the black/gray thread again and a decorative machine embroidery stitch that echoes the quilt's diagonal design. Lastly, outline the red sawtooth border triangles $1/4$ in/0.75 cm from the seam line using a black/red twisted rayon machine embroidery thread.

TIP

Use a walking/even-feed foot on your sewing machine when stitching through three or more layers to prevent tucks in the fabrics underneath.

---

5 Trim the excess batting and backing even with the quilt top.

6 Join the six black binding strips with diagonal seams to make a continuous length to fit all around the quilt and use to bind the edges with a double-fold binding, mitered at the corners. (See Continuous Strip Binding instructions on page 16.)

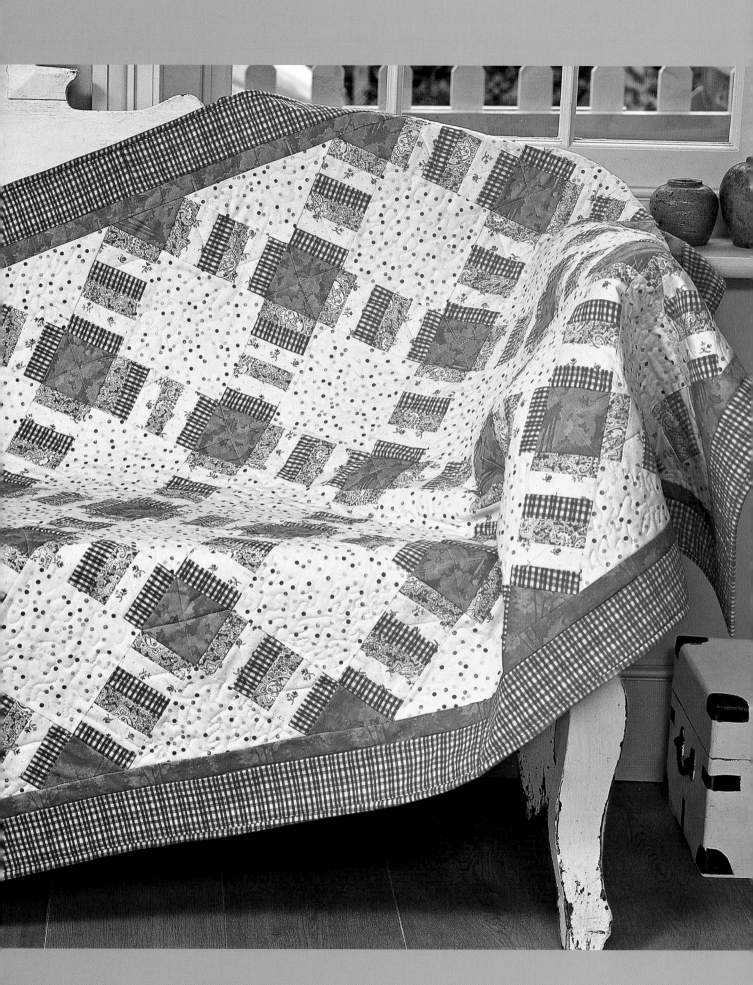

2. RAILROAD CROSSING

Designed by Janet Goddard

———

THIS SUMMERY QUILT uses a simple combination of fabric colors and patterns to create a vibrant design. The small prints, spots and checks in lemon, pink and green combine to produce a light, airy quilt that evokes memories of warm summer days and would be perfect to brighten up any room all year round.

———

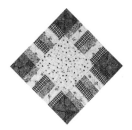

RAILROAD CROSSING

Quilt Plan

FINISHED SIZE: 46⅛ X 58⅞ IN/117 X 150 CM

MATERIALS

All fabrics used in the quilt top are 45 in/115 cm wide, 100% cotton. The backing fabric is 60 in/150 cm wide.

Large squares and large triangles:
lemon spot, 1 yard/1 m

Small rectangles: pink check, lemon print and pink swirl, ¹/₂ yard/40 cm of each

Small squares, triangles and inner border: green plain, ⁵/₈ yard/50 cm

Outer border and binding:
pink check, 1 yard/90 cm

Backing: 1³/₄ yards/1.6 m in color of your choice

Batting: 50 x 63 in/127 x 160 cm, 100% cotton

Thread: neutral cotton for piecing; lemon cotton for machine quilting

ALTERNATIVE COLOR SCHEMES

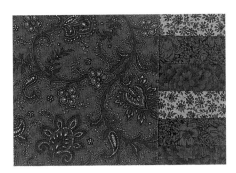

1 Bright colors suitable for a child's quilt.

2 Christmas prints with a hint of gold.

3 Classic patterns and shades for a traditional look.

4 Japanese-type fabrics with a two-color simple repeating pattern.

CUTTING

1 From the lemon spot fabric, cut eighteen 6¹/₂ in/17 cm squares. Cut two 5 in/13 cm squares and cross-cut these on the diagonal once to produce four triangles. Cut five 7¹/₄ in/19 cm squares and cross-cut these on the diagonal once to produce 10 triangles.

2 From each of the pink check, lemon print and pink swirl fabrics, cut 96 rectangles, 1¹/₂ x 3¹/₂ in/4 x 9 cm.

3 From the green plain fabric, cut seventeen 3¹/₂ in/9 cm squares. Cut seven 3⁷/₈ in/10 cm squares and cross-cut these on the diagonal once to produce 14 triangles. Cut five strips, 1¹/₂ in/4 cm deep, across the width of the fabric, for the inner border.

4 From the pink check fabric, cut seven strips, 3 in/8 cm deep, across the width of the fabric, for the outer border. Cut seven strips, 2 in/5 cm deep, across the width of the fabric, for the binding.

STITCHING

1 Use two rectangles of each fabric to make 48 six-rectangle blocks. Piece the strips together in the following order: pink check, lemon print, pink swirl, pink check, lemon print and pink swirl (*diagram 1*).

diagram 1

2 Stitch the rectangles together using a ¹/₄ in/0.75 cm seam allowance and press the seam allowances in one direction.

3 Following the quilt plan on page 28, lay out the pieced strips, the squares and triangles in 13 diagonal rows. Taking a ¹/₄ in/0.75 cm seam allowance, pin and stitch the blocks together in these diagonal rows. Press the seam allowances towards the large lemon spot squares and towards the small green squares and triangles.

4 Taking the usual seam allowance and matching the seams, pin and stitch the rows together to assemble the quilt.

ADDING THE BORDERS

1 To make the inner border, stitch three of the five 1¹/₂ in /4 cm green inner border strips into one continuous length. Measure the pieced top through the center from top to bottom and cut two strips to this measurement from the continuous length. (Discard the remainder of the continuous length.) Taking the usual seam allowance, pin and stitch to the sides of the quilt. Press the seam allowances towards the borders.

2 Measure the pieced top through the center from side to side and cut the remaining two inner border strips to this measurement. Taking the usual seam allowance, pin and stitch to the top and bottom of the quilt. Press the seam allowances towards the borders.

3 To make the outer border, join the seven 3 in/8 cm pink outer border strips into one continuous length. Repeat steps 1 and 2 using this length of stitched pink fabric to complete the outer border.

FINISHING

1 Spread the backing right side down on a flat surface, then smooth out the batting and the patchwork top, right side up, centrally on top. Fasten together with safety pins or baste in a grid.

2 Using the lemon thread, machine quilt a diagonal zigzag pattern along the pieced strips and across the small green squares (*diagram 2*). (For Machine Quilting instructions, see pages 14–15.)

diagram 2

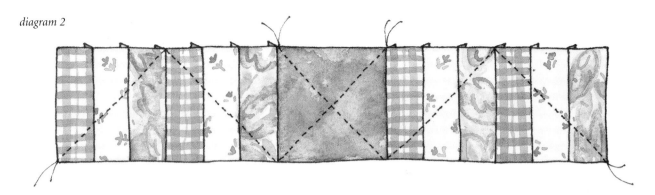

diagram 3

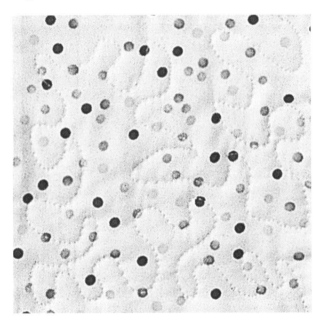

3 Machine quilt a large, random vermicelli-type pattern on the lemon spot squares (*diagram 3*).

4 Machine quilt in-the-ditch between the green inner border and the pink check outer border.

5 Trim any excess batting and backing even with the quilt top.

6 Join the seven binding strips with diagonal seams to make a continuous length to fit all around the quilt and use to bind the edges with a double-fold binding, mitered at the corners. (See Continuous Strip Binding instructions on page 16.)

3. FANS

Designed by Gail Smith

———

THIS QUILT COMPRISES 24 square blocks, which are turned onto a point. This arrangement calls for in-fill sections around all four sides of the quilt in which there is sashiko-style quilting, a type of Japanese quilt stitch meant to look like grains of rice. You can do the quilting by hand or machine. This quilt grows quickly, and doesn't take as long to make as you might think.

———

FANS

Quilt Plan

FINISHED SIZE: 67 1/2 X 84 1/2 IN / 172 X 215.5 CM

MATERIALS

All fabrics used in the quilt are 45 in/115 cm wide, 100% cotton.

Lightweight card stock

Fan segments: five different colors (green multi-batik, tan marble, dark turquoise, blue multi and dark green with gold detail), ⅝ yard/50 cm of each

Black quadrants and inner border: black marble with gold flecks, 1 yard/80 cm

Block background: pale lemon, 3 yards/2.6 m

In-fill sections: tan, 1¼ yards/1.1 m

Outer border and binding: a feature fabric, 1¼ yards/1.2 m (allow more for directional fabric)

Backing: 4 yards/3.5 m

Batting: 72 x 90 in/175 x 230 cm polyester

Thread: neutral thread for piecing; black and other dark cotton for decorative stitching and quilting

---

ALTERNATIVE COLOR SCHEMES

1 Bright florals for a bedroom.

2 Dark colors combined with more muted tones for a masculine look.

3 Bright mauves and pinks to cheer up any room.

4 Plain vibrant reds with patterned fabrics.

CUTTING

1 To cut the patchwork shapes, first make templates of lightweight card stock using the fan segment and quadrant-shaped templates on page 105. Cut 24 fan segments from each of the five fan fabrics by drawing around the template onto the back of the fabrics (the seam allowance is included).

2 From the black fabric, cut seven strips, 1½ in/4 cm deep, across the width of the fabric, for the inner border. Then cut out 24 quadrants using the card template as before.

3 From the lemon background fabric, cut eight strips, 12½ in/32 cm deep, across the width of the fabric. Cross-cut to produce a total of 24 x 12½ in /32 cm squares.

4 From the tan fabric for the in-fill sections, cut seven 12⅞ in/33 cm squares and cross-cut these on the diagonal once to produce 14 triangles. Cut one 8⅞ in/ 22.5 cm square, and again cross-cut on the diagonal once.

5 From the feature fabric, cut seven strips, 3 in/8 cm deep, across the width of the fabric, for the outer border. Cut eight strips, 2⅝ in/6.5 cm deep, across the width of the fabric, for the binding.

STITCHING

1 Taking a ¼ in/0.75 cm seam allowance, pin and stitch a set of fan segments together in the order

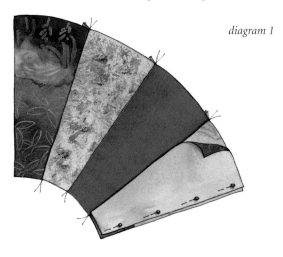

diagram 1

shown (*diagram 1*). Alternatively, stitch them together in pairs, as in chain piecing, then stitch the pairs together with the outer, fifth color. Continue until you have made all 24 fans. Press all the seam allowances in the same direction.

2 Pin the fans onto the lemon background blocks so that the outer edges of each fan are level with two edges of each block. Baste if desired. Machine stitch around each fan's long curve, very close to the edge. (The raw edges of the fabric are covered later at the quilting stage.)

3 Next pin the black quadrants in place, lining up the point of each quadrant with the corner of a fan block and overlapping the bottom of the fan. Baste if you prefer; then using black thread, zigzag stitch around the curved edge of the quadrant onto the block. You may now need to trim the fabric slightly just to neaten the blocks.

4 Following the quilt plan on page 34, lay out the fan blocks in six diagonal rows. Taking the usual seam allowance, pin then stitch the blocks together in these diagonal rows. Press the panel, pressing the seam allowances of Row 1 to the right, Row 2 to the left, Row 3 to the right, and so on.

5 Referring to the quilt plan and taking the usual seam allowance, stitch the in-fill triangles to the fan blocks. Stitch one of the two smaller triangles (cross-cut from the 8⅞ in/22.5 cm square) at the top of Row 3 and the other at the bottom of Row 4. For the top left and bottom right corners of the quilt stitch two of the 14 in-fill triangles together to make a larger one. Stitch the remaining 10 triangles to the ends of the rows as shown. Press the quilt, pressing the seams in alternating directions.

6 Starting at the top left corner, taking the usual seam allowance and matching the seams, pin and stitch the rows together to assemble the quilt. Where the seams have been pressed in alternate directions, a ridge should form to help you align the seams. Press the quilt top and trim it to leave a ⁵⁄₁₆ in/0.75 cm seam allowance all around, ready for joining the borders.

ADDING THE BORDERS

1 To make the inner border, stitch together the seven black inner border strips into one continuous length.

2 Measure the pieced top through the center from top to bottom and cut two strips to this measurement from the continuous length. Taking the usual seam allowance, pin and stitch to the sides of the quilt. Press the seam allowances towards the borders.

3 Measure the pieced top through the center from side to side and cut two strips to this measurement from the remaining continuous length. Join to the top and bottom of the quilt and press as before.

4 To make the outer border, join the seven 3 in/8 cm outer border strips into one continuous length. Repeating Steps 2 and 3, use this length of stitched fabric to complete the outer border.

TIP

A hand-quilted effect can be achieved on some sewing machines by using invisible thread on the bobbin – check your sewing machine manual.

FINISHING

1 Cut the backing fabric in half then stitch together along the long edges and press. Remove the selvages. Spread the backing right side down on a flat surface, then smooth out the batting and the patchwork top, right side up, on top. Fasten together with safety pins or baste in a grid.

2 Using dark thread and a walking foot, machine quilt around the fans and quadrants – use zigzag and fly stitch along the inner seams of the fans and satin stitch around the long outer edges of the fans. (See Machine Quilting instructions on page 14.)

3 Next quilt the in-fill sections. Using the fan segment template as a guide, draw quilting lines on the fabric with pencil, then quilt by hand or machine. Also apply quilting to the border if liked.

4 Trim excess batting and backing even with the quilt top.

5 Join the eight binding strips with diagonal seams to make a continuous length to fit all around the quilt and use to bind the edges with a double-fold binding, mitered at the corners. (See Continuous Strip Binding instructions on page 16.)

4. CLASSIC TULIPS

Designed by Janet Goddard

———

THIS APPLIQUÉD QUILT features a traditional tulip design worked in strong contrasting colors. The repeated tulip blocks in the center are offset with a border featuring further tulips, swags and corner ribbons and finished off with a bright yellow trim. Perfect as a wall hanging, lap quilt or sofa throw, the bold color scheme adds a contemporary twist to a classic design.

———

CLASSIC TULIPS

Quilt Plan

FINISHED SIZE: 40¾ IN/104 CM SQUARE

MATERIALS

All fabrics used in the quilt are 45 in/115 cm wide, 100% cotton.

Background: white print,
1 ¹/₂ yards/1.4 m

Tulip centers, inner and outer borders and binding:
yellow print, 1 yard/80 cm

Leaves, stems and swags:
green print, ¹/₂ yard/25 cm

Tulips: purple print, ¹/₂ yard/25 cm

Paper-backed fusible webbing:
40 in/102 cm

Backing: white print,
1 ¹/₄ yards/1.2 m

Batting: 45 x 45 in/115 x 115 cm,
80:20 cotton/polyester mix

Thread: neutral cotton for piecing; green, yellow and purple cotton to match appliqué fabrics; white cotton for hand quilting

---

ALTERNATIVE COLOR SCHEMES

1 Muted shades of blue, red and green.

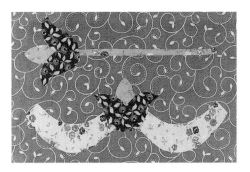

2 Hand-dyed fabrics in shades of orange and yellow.

3 Fresh, crisp prints in lime, peach and yellow.

4 A bold color scheme with a hint of Art Nouveau.

CUTTING

1 From the white background print, cut four 12¹/₂ in /32 cm squares, two 6¹/₂ x 26¹/₂ in/17 x 67 cm strips and two 6¹/₂ x 38¹/₂ in/17 x 98 cm strips.

2 From the yellow fabric, cut two 1¹/₂ x 24¹/₂ in/ 4 x 62 cm strips, two 1¹/₂ x 26¹/₂ in/4 x 67 cm strips, two 1¹/₂ x 38¹/₂ in/4 x 98 cm strips and two 1¹/₂ x 40¹/₂ in/4 x 103 cm strips. Cut four strips, 2 in/5 cm deep, across the width of the fabric, for the binding.

3 To cut the appliqué shapes, use the appliqué templates on page 105 and trace 36 tulips, 36 tulip centers, 16 leaves, eight stems, 20 swags and four of each ribbon on to fusible webbing. Cut out and iron on to the reverse of the appropriate fabric – tulips to the reverse of the purple fabric, tulip centers to the reverse of the yellow fabric, and leaves, stems, swags and ribbons to the reverse of the green fabric. Cut out all the shapes and set aside.

WORKING THE APPLIQUÉ

1 To make one of the four appliquéd center blocks, lightly fold a 12¹/₂ in/32 cm white background square on the diagonal twice so as to mark the center/orientation lines (*diagram 1*). Remove the backing paper from the reverse of two fused stem shapes. Position the stems along the diagonal lines, making sure the stems are centered equally, then iron in place.

diagram 1

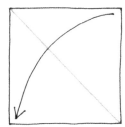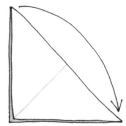

2 Remove the backing paper from the reverse of four fused leaf shapes and position each leaf in the center of the square between the stems and iron in place. Repeat this process with four tulip centers and four tulips, positioning a tulip at each end of a stem (*diagram 2*).

diagram 2

3 Zigzag stitch around each shape, matching the thread to the fabric.

4 Repeat Steps 1 to 3 to make four appliquéd center blocks in total.

STITCHING

1 Following the quilt plan on page 40, lay out the blocks in two rows of two blocks. Taking a ¹/₄ in/0.75 cm seam allowance, pin and stitch the blocks together in horizontal rows. Press the seam allowance in the first row in the opposite direction to the seam allowance in the second row.

2 Taking the usual seam allowance and matching the center seam, pin and stitch the two rows together.

ADDING THE BORDERS

1 To make the inner border, stitch the 1¹/₂ x 24¹/₂ in /4 x 62 cm yellow strips to the top and bottom of the center panel. Press the seam allowances towards the borders.

2 Stitch the 1¹/₂ x 26¹/₂ in/4 x 67 cm yellow strips to each side of the center panel. Press the seam allowances towards the borders.

3 To make the appliquéd border, stitch the 6¹/₂ x 26¹/₂ in /17 x 67 cm white background strips to the top and bottom of the center panel. Press the seam allowances towards the borders.

4 Stitch the $6^{1}/_{2}$ x $38^{1}/_{2}$ in/17 x 98 cm white background strips to each side of the center panel. Press the seam allowances towards the borders.

5 Now add the remaining fused appliqué shapes to the white background border. Position five swags and four tulips along each side of the quilt. Ensure these are evenly spaced, and that a tulip covers both ends of each swag. Position a tulip on each corner of the quilt, again ensuring that the tulip covers the ends of the swags. Position a pair of ribbons under each corner tulip (*diagram 3*). When all shapes are positioned correctly, remove the backing paper from the reverse of each shape and iron in place.

diagram 3

6 Zigzag stitch around each shape, matching the thread to the fabric.

7 To make the outer border, stitch the $1^{1}/_{2}$ x $38^{1}/_{2}$ in/ 4 x 98 cm yellow strips to the top and bottom of the quilt. Press the seam allowances towards the borders.

8 Lastly, stitch the $1^{1}/_{2}$ x $40^{1}/_{2}$ in/4 x 103 cm yellow strips to each side of the quilt. Press the seam allowances towards the borders.

FINISHING

1 Spread the backing right side down on a flat surface, then smooth out the batting and the patchwork top, right side up, on top. Fasten together with safety pins or baste in a grid.

2 Using the white quilting thread, hand quilt $1/_{4}$ in/0.75 cm around each appliqué shape. (See Hand Quilting instructions on page 15.) Quilt $1/_{4}$ in/0.75 cm in from the seam lines on each side of the yellow border strips so that the quilting lies on the white fabric (*diagram 4*).

diagram 4

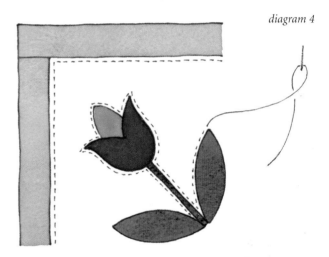

3 Rule a 2 in/5 cm grid using a marked pencil over the quilt on the diagonal ensuring that the center diagonal lines cross through the center of the quilt. Quilt on the drawn lines.

4 Trim any excess batting and backing even with the quilt top.

5 Join the binding strips with diagonal seams to make a continuous length to fit all around the quilt and use to bind the edges with a double-fold binding, mitered at the corners. (See Continuous Strip Binding instructions on page 16.)

5. QUERCUS AUTUMNALIS

Designed by Andrea McMillan

———

THIS QUILT IS BASED on a traditional appliqué design called "Oak Leaf and Reel" so I've named it after the Latin name for the Oak. It features hand appliqué using classic autumnal-colored fabrics with four of the 13 blocks having a simple stitched outline. A quicker and simpler version could be made by fusing the appliqué shapes in place.

———

QUERCUS AUTUMNALIS
Quilt Plan

FINISHED SIZE: 54 ¾ X 54 ¾ IN/137.5 X 137.5 CM

MATERIALS

All fabrics used in the quilt top are 45 in/115 cm wide, 100% cotton. The backing fabric is 60 in/150 cm wide.

Background and borders:
cream print, 2¼ yards/2.25 m

Oak leaf and reel appliqué:
autumnal-colored fabrics, nine fat quarters of assorted squares

Accent border and binding:
rust-colored print, ⅝ yard/50 cm

Lightweight card stock: 10 in/ 25 cm square

Darning needle

Backing: 1 ⅝ yards/1.4 m in color of your choice

Batting: 55 x 55 in/140 x 140 cm

Thread: four colors of perlé thread to match appliqué fabrics

---

ALTERNATIVE COLOR SCHEMES

1 Patterned fabrics on a plain muted background.

2 Bright mauves and blues.

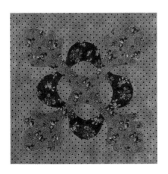

3 A pairing of pinks and greens.

4 Red and green for a Christmas feel.

CUTTING

1 From the cream background print, cut four 5$^1/_2$ x 55 in/14 x 140 cm strips from the length of the fabric for the border, and cut 13 x 10$^1/_2$ in/27 cm squares for the appliquéd background. Cut two 15$^1/_2$ in/39.5 cm squares, then cross-cut them twice on the diagonal to produce eight triangles for the sides of the quilt. Cut two 8$^1/_2$ in/22 cm squares, then cross-cut them to produce four triangles for the quilt's corners.

2 To cut the appliqué shapes, make a template of lightweight card stock using the appliqué templates on page 106. Cut one oak leaf appliqué and four reels from each of the autumnal fabrics by placing the template on the back of the fabric and drawing around it with a pencil. With the template still in place, use the darning needle to firmly mark around the outline — this helps to turn in the edge of the appliqué when stitching. Cut out the pieces, cutting $^1/_4$ in/0.75 cm outside the pencil line. Snip into the seam allowance on the curves.

3 From the rust-colored print, cut four 1 in/2.5 cm strips across the width of the fabric, for the accent border. Cut five 2$^1/_2$ in/6.5 cm strips across the width of the fabric, for the binding.

STITCHING

1 To make one of the nine appliquéd blocks, each with contrasting oak leaf and reels, place the oak leaf shape centrally on the background square with the four reel shapes positioned with their ends tucked under. Stitch the reels in place first, using tiny stitches to secure them to the background square and tucking under the seam allowance as you go. Stitch the oak leaf shape in the same way. Repeat the process to complete the other eight appliquéd blocks.

2 Stitch the four remaining background squares with an outline of the design in perlé thread. Using the appliqué templates, mark the design centrally on the back of each background square with a pencil. Using your chosen perlé thread, stitch around the outline with small running stitches, using the pencil line as a guide. (This can be stitched from the back to make it easier to follow the lines.)

3 To join the blocks, lay out the appliquéd and stitched squares and the side and corner triangle pieces as shown in *diagram 1*. Taking a $^1/_4$ in/0.75 cm seam allowance, pin and stitch the pieces together in diagonal strips. Stitch the strips together, taking the usual seam allowance and matching the seams. Press the seam allowance in the first row in the opposite direction to that in the second row, and so on, to reduce the bulk in the seams.

diagram 1

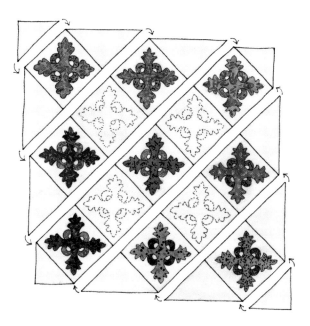

ADDING THE BORDERS

1 To make the accent border, measure the pieced top through the center from side to side, then cut two of the four 1 in/2.5 cm strips to this measurement. Stitch to the top and bottom of the quilt. Next measure the pieced top through the center from top to bottom, then cut the remaining two strips to this measurement. Stitch to the sides. Press the seam allowances towards the darker fabric.

2 Measuring the pieced top through the center in the same way, cut the four strips for the main border to length and stitch in place to each side. Again, press the seam allowances towards the darker fabric.

FINISHING

1 Spread the backing right side down on a flat surface, then smooth out the batting and the patchwork top, right side up, centrally on top. Fasten together with safety pins or baste in a grid.

2 Machine or hand quilt ¼ in/0.75 cm around each appliqué shape and stitched outline, as well as in parallel lines around the edge of the quilt and across the triangles in the center panel. (For Quilting instructions, see pages 14–15.)

3 Join the binding strips with diagonal seams to make a continuous length to fit all around the quilt and use to bind the edges with a double-fold binding, mitered at the corners. (See Continuous Strip Binding instructions on page 16.)

6. TWIRLING ROSE OF SHARON
Designed by Sarah Fincken

FABRICS IN WARM GOLDS, soft yellows, rusts and greens combine with a cream and white background fabric to make this updated version of a traditional roses block pattern. Twirling roses and stems around a center rose create a spinning visual effect, which makes the roses appear to dance across the whole surface of the quilt, even though each block is surrounded by a strip of green sashing. Any choice of color palette suits this design. You could use up lots of scraps left over from other projects for the flowers, leaves and stems, but it's best to unify the different blocks by using just one or two key fabrics for every block.

TWIRLING ROSE OF SHARON

Quilt Plan

FINISHED SIZE: 57 X 71 IN/142.5 X 177.5 CM

MATERIALS

All fabrics used in the quilt top are 45 in/115 cm wide, 100% cotton. The backing fabric is 90 in/2.3 m wide.

Block background and border fabric: white/cream, 3⅝ yards/3.2 m

Sashing strips and binding: mid-green, 2⅝ yards/2.4 m

Rose stems: dark green with rust and gold spots, ¾ yard/70 cm

Leaves and buds: mid- and dark green spotted fabrics, scraps to total ¾ yard/70 cm

Frilly petals: rust/yellow/green stripe, ½ yard/30 cm

Large roses: six different yellows/golds, ¼ yard/25 cm of each

Small roses, small center roses and buds: Pieces of assorted yellow/gold/rust plain and patterned fabrics, no smaller than 3 in/8 cm square – to total ¾ yard/70 cm

Large and small central rose circles: Pieces of assorted yellow/gold/rust plain and patterned fabrics, no smaller than 2½ in/6.5 cm square – to total 1 yard/1 m

Paper-backed fusible webbing: 1½ yards/137 cm

Baking parchment

Backing: 1¾ yards/1.6 m in color of your choice

Batting: 60 x 74 in/152 x 188 cm, 80:20 cotton/polyester

Thread: green, yellow and orange cotton to match appliqué fabrics; neutral cotton for piecing; invisible thread, cream, mid-green and golden cotton for quilting

---

ALTERNATIVE COLOR SCHEMES

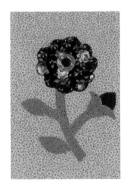

1 Floral prints in muted tones for a "folk art" feel.

2 An Amish color palette against a plain background for a dramatic scheme with a contemporary look.

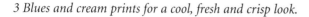

3 Blues and cream prints for a cool, fresh and crisp look.

4 Patterned fabrics on a muted background for a soft feel.

CUTTING

1 From the white/cream print, cut two 7$\frac{1}{2}$ x 50 in /19 x 127 cm strips and two 7$\frac{1}{2}$ x 74 in/19 x 188 cm strips for the borders. Cut twelve 13 in/33 cm squares for the blocks.

2 From the mid-green patterned sashing fabric, cut the following pieces:
- eight strips, 2$\frac{1}{2}$ x 12$\frac{1}{2}$ in/6.5 x 31.5 cm.
- five strips, 2$\frac{1}{2}$ x 40$\frac{1}{2}$ in/6.5 x 101.5 cm.
- two strips, 2$\frac{1}{2}$ x 58$\frac{1}{2}$ in/6.5 x 146.5 cm.
- six strips, 2$\frac{1}{2}$ in/6.5 cm deep, across the width of the fabric, for the binding.

3 From the dark green fabric with rust and gold spots, cut $\frac{5}{8}$ in/1.5 cm strips on the bias for the binding for the rose stems, until you have cut up all the fabric.

4 To cut the appliqué shapes, use a pencil and the appliqué templates on page 106 and trace 48 rose buds, 48 leaf buds and 208 leaves onto the paper side of the fusible webbing, plus all the pattern pieces required to make 16 large and 58 small rose units.

5 Cut out all the fusible webbing shapes, cutting approximately $\frac{1}{4}$ in/0.75 cm outside the penciled line each time. For the larger shapes such as the rose outlines, cut away the middle of the webbing (this keeps the fabric more supple and allows the quilting to puff out

the shapes). To do this, make a snip in the middle of each motif and trim the fusible webbing to $\frac{1}{4}$ in/0.75 cm away from the inside of the penciled line.

6 Place each cut shape, paper side up, onto the reverse of the appropriate fabric. (Note, 48 of the leaves should be cut from dark green spotted fabric for the blocks, the remaining leaves from mid-green spotted fabric for the blocks and borders.) Cover each shape with a piece of baking parchment and fuse in place with a medium hot iron. Cut out along the penciled line to achieve the exact shape.

WORKING THE APPLIQUÉ

1 Start by preparing the bias binding strips for the rose stems. Finger press the bias binding strips into three equal sections along the length. Fold the side sections to the back, slightly overlapping the edges at the center back, so the right side of the fabric is on the outside of the folded "tube" (*diagram 1*). Baste along the center line to hold the raw edges in position before pressing the strip.

diagram 1

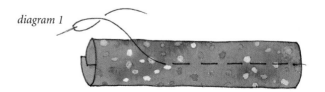

diagram 2

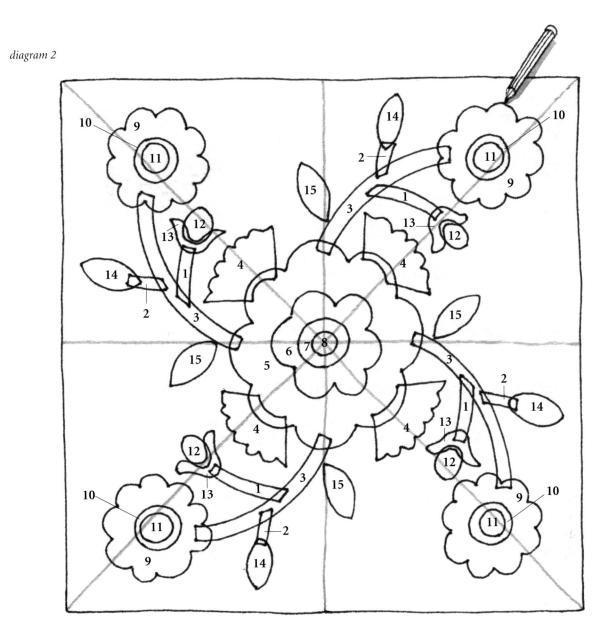

2 For the appliquéd center blocks, first make a paper template to help you position the shapes correctly on the background square. Cut a 12 in/30 cm square (the finished block size) out of tracing paper. Fold the square into quarters and then fold in half on the diagonal to form a triangle. Unfold the paper then, using a pen, mark the appliqué motifs on the paper (*diagram 2*), starting with the outer central rose shape (no. 5) and the bias binding rose stems (nos. 1, 2 and 3), making sure that the raw ends of the bias stems extend so that they can be tucked underneath each shape.

3 Now press all 12 background fabric blocks, marking the center/orientation lines by making the same crease marks as you did in the paper template.

4 Position the paper template centrally on one of the background fabric blocks and secure at each corner with pins while you position the bias binding strips, cutting them to the correct length as you go. Remove the template and baste the bias binding stems in position.

TIP

Use a rotary cutting set to cut all your strips and squares of the fabric on the straight of grain. The border strips and blocks have an extra 1 in/2.5 cm added to their finished size to allow for extra fabric being taken up when stitching the appliqué motifs. The blocks and border strips are trimmed to their exact unfinished size with 1/4 in/0.75 cm seam allowances when stitched.

5 Now apply the rest of the appliqué shapes, working from the back of the design to the front because of the layering of motifs. Remove the backing paper from the reverse of the fused frilly petals (no. 4). Using the paper template again as a guide, place them in position then, using baking parchment on top, iron in place. Repeat this process with the outer large rose and then the rest of the appliqué motifs.

6 Stitch the rose stem binding in place using green thread and a straight machine stitch down either side of the bias binding as near to the edge as possible. Always stitch the inner curve first. Machine zigzag stitch around the raw edge of each appliqué shape, matching the thread to the fabric.

7 Repeat Steps 4 to 6 to make 12 appliquéd center blocks in total. Make sure that you choose a mixture of yellow, gold and rust fabrics and green leaves for each individual block.

8 Now appliqué the border strips. Fold the four cream border strips in half and mark each center with a pin, placing the pin 2 in/5 cm from what will be the inner edge of each border strip. For the two side border strips measure 14 in/36 cm either side of the center pin and place two more pins as before, so as to mark the position of all three roses. For the border strips for the top and bottom of the quilt, place a pin 7 in/18 cm either side of the center, so as to mark the position of the two roses.

9 Cut the remaining prepared bias binding strips into 14 lengths of 16 in/40 cm for the border rose stems. For the top and bottom borders place one end of the binding in line with one pin and then curve the binding in a gentle arc to reach the point of the next pin, pinning in place along the inside of the curve and taking care not to stretch the binding. Stitch. Pin then stitch the adjoining outer lengths of binding only as far as the middle of the arc (these will be stitched down later). Repeat for the side border strips.

10 Following the quilt plan on page 52, arrange the leaves and roses in place. Fuse then zigzag stitch as before (Step 6 above). Don't yet add the final sets of four leaves and the corner roses or stitch down the corner stems. This is done only after you have joined the borders to the sashed panel, as the rest of the corner arc of binding forms slightly less of a curve and the raw ends tuck behind the corner large roses. (See "Adding the Borders," Step 3.)

STITCHING

1 Using a rotary cutting set, trim the 12 appliqué blocks so that each one measures $12\frac{1}{2}$ in/31.5 cm square with a large rose in the center. You can now start joining the blocks and sashing strips together, following the quilt plan on page 52.

2 Take the eight $2\frac{1}{2}$ x $12\frac{1}{2}$ in/6.5 x 31.5 cm strips of mid-green sashing fabric and align one long edge of each strip, right sides facing, with the right hand edge of eight appliqué blocks. Pin then stitch together, taking a $\frac{1}{4}$ in/0.75 cm seam allowance. Next, join two sashed blocks together along a vertical edge, taking the usual seam allowance. Add an unsashed block to each right hand edge to form four rows of three vertically sashed blocks.

3 Take three of the five $2\frac{1}{2}$ x $40\frac{1}{2}$ in/6.5 x 101.5 cm strips of mid-green sashing fabric and align one long edge, right sides facing, with the bottom edge of three of the sashed rows. Pin then stitch together, taking the usual seam allowance. Pin and stitch the four rows together to complete the internal sashing of the center panel.

4 Pin then stitch the remaining two $2\frac{1}{2}$ x $40\frac{1}{2}$ in/6.5 x 101.5 cm strips of mid-green sashing fabric to the top and bottom of the center panel, taking the usual seam allowance. Lastly, stitch the two $2\frac{1}{2}$ x $58\frac{1}{2}$ in/6.5 x 146.5 cm strips to the sides of the panel, then press. The completed sashed center panel now measures $44\frac{1}{2}$ x $58\frac{1}{2}$ in/111.5 x 146.5 cm.

TIP

When cutting out fused motifs you can achieve a smoother, more accurate shape if you keep your scissor hand stationary and use your other hand to turn the fused fabric, guiding it into the scissor blades so that they cut exactly along the penciled line.

ADDING THE BORDERS

1 Trim the long edge of the border strips nearest the roses to leave 1 in/2.5 cm below each rose. Then align your ruler with this straightened edge and trim the border width to 6¹/₂ in/16.5 cm.

2 Taking the usual seam allowance, pin and stitch the shorter border strips to the top and bottom of the center panel, making sure each small rose is aligned with the middle of the vertical sashing strips and taking care not to catch the loose ends of the bias binding stems in your stitching by mistake. Trim the ends of the border strips in line with the center panel but do not trim off any of the binding strip. Press the seams to one side.

3 Pin and stitch the remaining two border strips to each side of the center panel. Position, pin then stitch the corner bias binding rose stems in place to make gentle curved corners (see quilt plan). Fuse the large corner roses and the remaining border leaves in position and complete the appliqué with machine zigzag stitching as before.

FINISHING

1 Spread the backing right side down on a flat surface, then smooth out the batting and the patchwork top, right side up, centrally on top. Fasten together with safety pins or baste in a grid.

2 Using a walking foot, a stitch length of 3.5, invisible thread on the spool and cream thread to match the backing fabric on the bobbin, machine quilt in-the-ditch using a "hand quilting" machine stitch around the blocks and inner border. (For In-the-Ditch Machine Quilting instructions, see page 15 and diagram 17.)

3 Use a chalk marker and the quilting templates on page 107 to mark the leaf vine pattern on all the green sashing and border strips. Using green quilting thread, hand quilt this design on all the green strips. Using cream quilting thread, hand quilt ¹/₄ in/0.75 cm around each appliquéd shape in the blocks and border. Lastly, hand quilt the outer yellow large rose centers using golden quilting cotton.

4 Trim any excess batting and backing even with the quilt top.

5 Join the six mid-green binding strips with diagonal seams to make a continuous length to fit all around the quilt and use to bind the edges with a double-fold binding, mitered at the corners. (See Continuous Strip Binding instructions on page 16.)

7. BLOOMS, BASKETS AND BLUEBIRDS

Designed by Janet Goddard

THE BLUEBIRD MOTIF IS a traditional design often found in appliquéd quilts. In this quilt each of the four baskets features two bluebirds and a variety of flowers and leaves, which are positioned differently in each basket. The flowers and bluebirds are in soft muted colors and the design extends to the outer border. This small quilt is machine appliquéd and hand quilted but could easily be hand appliquéd, too. It would make an ideal lap quilt, or a throw for a favorite chair.

BLOOMS, BASKETS AND BLUEBIRDS

Quilt Plan

FINISHED SIZE: 28 ¾ X 28 ¾ IN / 73 X 73 CM

MATERIALS

All fabrics used in the quilt are 45 in/115 cm wide, 100% cotton.

Background: white print,
1/2 yard/30 cm

Inner border and binding: dark peach, 1/2 yard/33 cm

Outer border: blue floral,
1/2 yard/40 cm

Baskets: blue check, 1/2 yard/25 cm

Bluebirds: blue spot, 1/4 yard/10 cm

Bluebird wings: blue floral,
1/4 yard/5 cm

Leaves: green print and green spot,
1/4 yard/5 cm of each

Flowers: four peach-colored fabrics graded from light to dark,
1/4 yard/8 cm of each

Paper-backed fusible webbing:
25 in/64 cm

Backing: 1 yard/90 cm

Batting: 32 x 32 in/81 x 81 cm

Thread: neutral cotton for piecing; blue, green and peach cotton to match appliqué fabrics; white cotton for hand quilting; navy blue embroidery thread for bluebirds' eyes

---

ALTERNATIVE COLOR SCHEMES

1 Classic muted tones for a traditional feel.

2 Spots and flowers—a stunning combination.

3 Bright blues, pinks and greens to suit a child's bedroom.

4 Creams, browns and reds with a hint of gold.

CUTTING

1 From the white background print, cut four 10^1/$_2$ in/ 27 cm squares.

2 From the dark peach fabric, cut two 1^1/$_2$ x 20^1/$_2$ in/ 4 x 52.5 cm strips and two 1^1/$_2$ x 22^1/$_2$ in/4 x 57.5 cm strips for the inner border. Cut four 2 x 29 in/5.5 x 74 cm strips for the binding.

3 From the blue floral print, cut two 3^1/$_2$ x 22^1/$_2$ in/9 x 57.5 cm strips and two 3^1/$_2$ x 28^1/$_2$ in/9 x 72.5 cm strips for the outer border.

4 To cut the appliqué shapes, use the appliqué templates on page 107 and trace four baskets, 12 bluebirds (six facing each way), 12 bluebird wings (six facing each way), 44 leaves, 20 flower 1s plus centers, eight flower 2s plus centers, eight flower 3s plus centers and 12 flower 4s plus centers on to fusible webbing. Cut out and iron on to the reverse of the appropriate fabric. Use one of the four peach fabrics for each different flower type (i.e. flower 1, 2, 3 and 4). Also cut the flower centers from these four peach fabrics. Iron 24 fusible webbing leaves on to the green spot fabric and 20 leaves to the green print. Lastly, when ironing the fusible webbing basket shapes to the blue check fabric, position the baskets on a slight angle so that the check pattern is on the diagonal. Cut out all the shapes and set aside.

WORKING THE APPLIQUÉ

1 To make one of the four appliquéd center blocks, take a 10^1/$_2$ in/27 cm white background square and a fused basket shape. Remove the backing paper from the reverse of the basket. Position the basket on the background square, ^{3}/$_4$ in/2 cm up from the bottom edge, then iron in place.

2 Remove the backing paper from two bluebirds and their wings (one bluebird facing each way), six leaves, three flower 1s, two flower 2s, two flower 3s, three flower 4s and their corresponding flower centers. Position all the fused shapes in and around the basket (*diagram 1*). Iron in place.

diagram 1

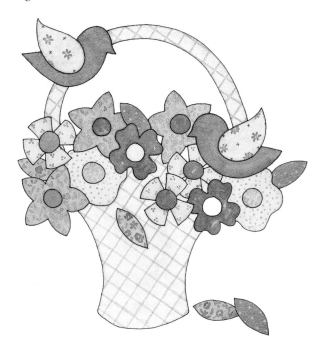

3 Zigzag stitch around each shape, matching the thread to the fabric.

4 Using the navy blue embroidery thread, stitch a French knot on each bluebird's head to represent its eye.

5 Repeat Steps 1 to 4 to make four appliquéd center blocks in total. Refer to the quilt plan on page 60 for positioning – although each block has the same number of leaves, flowers and bluebirds, these are positioned differently in each block.

STITCHING

1 Following the quilt plan on page 60, lay out the four appliquéd blocks in two rows of two blocks. Taking a ^{1}/$_4$ in/0.75 cm seam allowance, pin and stitch the blocks together in horizontal rows.

2 Taking the usual seam allowance and matching the center seams, pin and stitch the two rows together.

ADDING THE BORDERS

1 To make the inner border, stitch the $1^1/_2$ x $20^1/_2$ in/ 4 x 52.5 cm dark peach strips to each side of the center panel. Press the seam allowances towards the borders.

2 Stitch the $1^1/_2$ x $22^1/_2$ in/4 x 57.5 cm dark peach strips to the top and bottom of the center panel. Press the seam allowances towards the borders.

3 To make the appliquéd outer border, stitch the $3^1/_2$ x $22^1/_2$ in/9 x 57.5 cm blue floral strips to each side of the center panel. Press the seam allowances towards the border.

4 Stitch the $3^1/_2$ x $28^1/_2$ in/9 x 72.5 cm blue floral strips to the top and bottom of the center panel. Press the seam allowances towards the borders.

5 Now add the remaining fused appliqué shapes to the blue border. Position five leaves, one bluebird and two flowers in each corner of the quilt. Ensure that the leaves overlap each other and that the bluebird sits on top of the leaves (see the quilt plan for positioning). When all shapes are positioned correctly, remove the backing paper from the reverse of each shape and iron in place.

6 Zigzag stitch around each shape, matching the thread to the fabric. Stitch a French knot for each bluebird's eye, as before.

FINISHING

1 Spread the backing right side down on a flat surface, then smooth out the batting and the patchwork top, right side up, centrally on top. Fasten together with safety pins or baste in a grid.

2 Using the white quilting thread, hand quilt $^1/_4$ in/ 0.75 cm around each appliqué shape. (See Hand Quilting instructions on page 15.) Quilt $^1/_4$ in/0.75 cm in from the seam lines on the white background center panel and on the dark peach border strip. Use a light pencil and the quilting template on page 107 to trace the outline of three flowers and two leaves on to the mid-section of each length of blue border, then quilt by hand.

3 Outline quilt a second row of stitches $^1/_2$ in/1 cm away from the first row of quilting around each shape. Quilt four bluebirds on the outer edge of the background square positioning the birds on the seam lines. Using the templates from the appliqué, quilt six flowers in a random fashion in the center of the quilt.

4 Trim the excess batting and backing even with the quilt top.

5 Use the four dark peach binding strips to bind the edges of the quilt with a double-fold binding. Attach a length of binding to each side of the quilt first, then use the remaining two lengths at the top and bottom of the quilt. (See instructions for Binding the Four Sides Separately on page 17.)

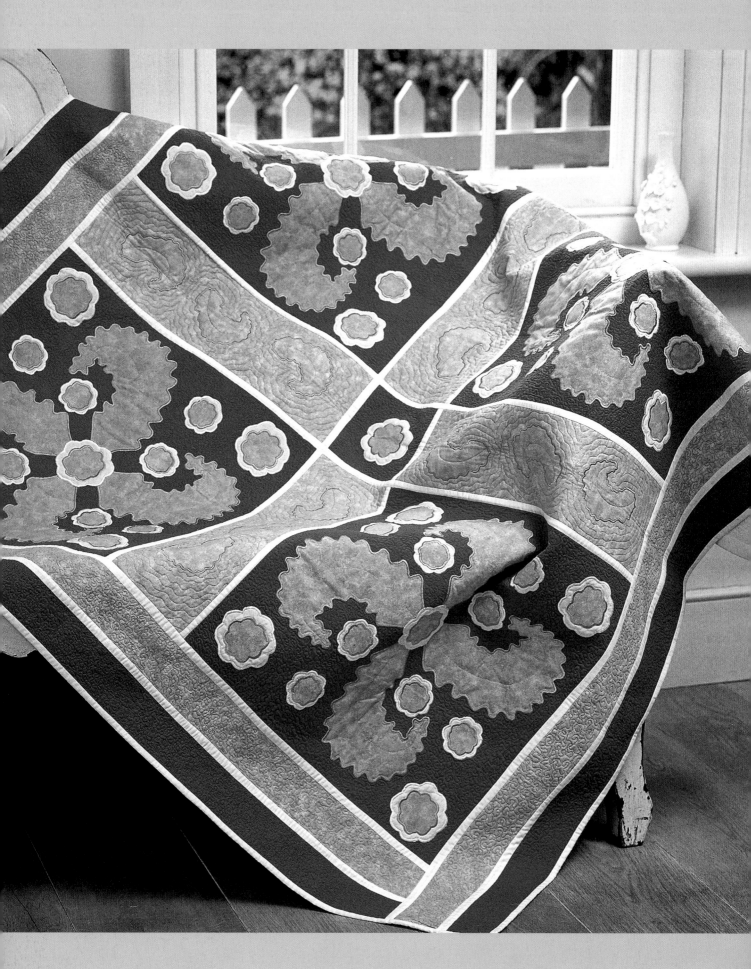

8. PRINCESS FEATHER

Designed by Natalia Manley

———

THIS QUILT HAS BEEN DESIGNED as a "quilt as you go" project. To allow for possible fabric shrinkage while machine quilting, I have planned a generous 2 in/5 cm surplus fabric all around each block and border. All the individually quilted blocks and borders are then assembled using white joining strips, which are an integral part of the design.

———

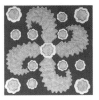

PRINCESS FEATHER

Quilt Plan

FINISHED SIZE: 61 X 61 IN/155.5 X 155.5 CM

MATERIALS

All fabrics used in the quilt top are 45 in/115 cm wide, 100% cotton.

Four large blocks, central square and outer borders:
mid-blue, 3 yards/2.6 m

Feathers, flowers, central strips and inner borders:
pale blue, 4 yards/3.5 m

Joining strips, flowers and binding: white, 4 yards/3.5 m

Backing: 7 yards/6.5 m

Paper-backed fusible webbing: approximately 3¹/₄ yards/3 m

Medium/firm weight tear-away stabilizer: enough to cover each motif to be appliquéd

Batting: 7 yards/6.5 m cotton

Thread: blue, pale blue and white machine embroidery thread; sewing thread and bobbin thread to match backing fabric

---

ALTERNATIVE COLOR SCHEMES

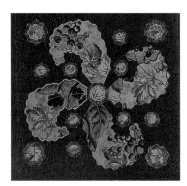

1 Muted warm tones.

2 Vibrant oranges and yellows.

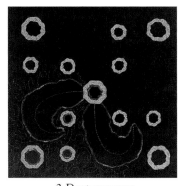

3 Deep mauves.

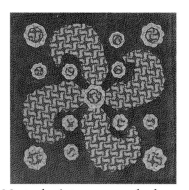

4 Mustard prints on a green background.

CUTTING

1 From the mid-blue fabric, cut the following pieces:
 • four 25 x 25 in/64 x 64 cm blocks.
 • one 10 x 10 in/25 x 25 cm square, for the center.
 • one 17 x 64 in/43 x 163 cm strip, for the outer border.

2 From the pale blue fabric, cut the following pieces:
 • four 25 x 10 in/64 x 25 cm rectangles, for the central strips.
 • one 17 x 64 in/43 x 163 cm strip, for the inner border.
 • (The remainder of the pale blue fabric is for the appliqué flowers.)

3 From the backing fabric and the batting, cut the following pieces:
 • four 25 x 25 in/64 x 64 cm blocks.
 • one 10 x 10 in/25 x 25 cm square.
 • two 17 x 64 in/43 x 163 cm strips.
 • four 25 x 10 in/64 x 25 cm rectangles.

4 From the white fabric, cut two $2^1/2$ x 60 in/6.5 x 152 cm strips and two $2^1/2$ x 63 in/6.5 x 160 cm strips, for the binding and set aside. Cut the following pieces for the joining strips:
 • four 1 x 21 in/3 x 53 cm strips, and four $1^1/2$ x 21 in/4.5 x 53 cm strips.
 • two 1 x 6 in/3 x 15 cm strips, and two $1^1/2$ x 6 in/4.5 x 15 cm strips.
 • six 1 x 48 in/3 x 122 cm strips, and six $1^1/2$ x 48 in/4.5 x 122 cm strips.
 • four 1 x 60 in/3 x 152 cm strips, and four $1^1/2$ x 60 in/4.5 x 152 cm strips.
 • (The remainder of the white fabric is for the appliqué flowers.)

5 To cut the appliqué shapes, use the appliqué templates on page 108 and trace 16 feathers, 21 large flowers, 53 medium flowers and 32 small flowers on to fusible webbing. Cut out and iron on to the reverse of the appropriate fabric – 21 large flowers and 32 medium flowers to the reverse of the remaining white fabric, and the 16 feathers, 21 medium flowers and 32 small flowers to the reverse of the remaining pale blue fabric. Carefully cut out all the shapes and set aside.

WORKING THE APPLIQUÉ

1 To make the four large appliquéd blocks, fold each 25 x 25 in/64 x 64 cm mid-blue square twice and lightly press so as to mark the center/orientation lines.

2 Using a light pencil and the positional template on page 108, trace the block design on to each square, matching the center/orientation lines with the ironed lines on the square. Use a light box or a light source such as a window to help trace the design.

3 Working on one block at a time, carefully remove the backing paper from the reverse of each motif and position carefully on the block, ironing each piece in place as you work. Start by placing the feathers, then the central flower and finally all the remaining flowers. Prepare all four blocks in the same way.

4 Prepare the 10 x 10 in/25 x 25 cm mid-blue central square in exactly the same way as each large block and set aside.

5 The five blocks are now ready for machine appliqué. Prepare each one either by backing with tear-away stabilizer or by using the batting/stabilizer method described in the tip box (below).

6 Using a medium width, $1/8$ in/3 – 4 mm, satin stitch throughout, start by stitching around the outline of each feather using pale blue machine embroidery thread. Next, stitch around all the inner flowers. Finally, using white machine embroidery thread, satin stitch around all the white flowers.

TIP

For satin stitch (i.e. a tight zigzag stitch), it is essential to back the motif to be appliquéd with a good stabilizer, preferably a tear-away medium or firm weight one. This stops the fabric from puckering and helps create a smooth appliqué line. However, I recommend backing the block to be appliquéd first with cotton batting and then with stabilizer to create an "appliqué quilt sandwich." This works beautifully, creating a quilted effect as you stitch and helping the needle glide through all the layers. Satin stitch done in this way is particularly dense and attractive.

7 When you have completed the stitching, carefully remove all the stabilizer from the back of the blocks. Tidy up any loose ends of thread by taking them through to the back of the appliquéd blocks using a wide-eyed needle.

QUILTING

1 Place a 25 x 25 in/64 x 64 cm square of backing right side down on a flat surface. If you haven't already used batting for the appliqué, place a 25 x 25 in/64 x 64 cm square of batting on top. Lastly, place one of the four large appliquéd blocks, right side up, on top. Pin or baste together through all the layers and zigzag around the outer edges to minimize shrinkage during quilting and to hold all the layers together. Back the other three large appliquéd blocks in the same way.

2 Using pale blue machine embroidery thread, quilt the inside of each feather (*diagram 1*). If liked, you could also quilt the flowers in the middle of each feather block. To do this, start in the center of each flower and embroider petal shapes to create a daisy outline, returning to the center each time you complete a petal. Using mid-blue embroidery thread and a vermicelli quilting stitch (for example, see page 15), apply free motion quilting over the background of each block.

diagram 1

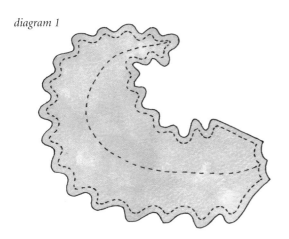

3 Back the 10 x 10 in/25 x 25 cm mid-blue central square and stitch the background in the same way.

4 Now quilt the borders, quilting them in one large piece before cutting them up into strips. Back the pale blue and the mid-blue 17 x 64 in/43 x 163 cm fabric pieces with batting and backing fabric as per Step 1 above. As before, pin or baste together through all the layers and zigzag around the outer edges.

5 Using machine embroidery thread to match the fabric, quilt each piece with a vermicelli stitch. Because the four border strips to be cut from each of these pieces are of different lengths – two are 60 in/ 152 cm and two are 48 in/122 cm long – quilt half the piece lengthways to around only 50 in/127 cm long, but do not cut off any excess fabric at this stage.

6 To quilt the pale blue central strips, use a light pencil and the quilting template on page 108 to trace the outline of three small feathers on to each strip. Prepare the "quilt appliqué sandwich" as before (see tip above). Using a $^1/_8$ in/3 – 4 mm wide satin stitch, carefully stitch around the outline of each feather. When completed remove the tear-away stabilizer and tidy up any loose ends of thread as before. (Alternatively, simply quilt the outline of the feathers using a straight machine stitch.)

7 Back the central strips as before (Step 1, "Quilting"). Apply free motion quilting over the background of each strip using pale blue machine embroidery thread and contour quilting, also known as echo or Hawaiian quilting (*diagram 2*). (See also Echo Quilting on page 15, diagram 18.)

diagram 2

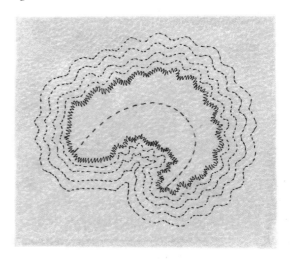

STITCHING

diagram 3

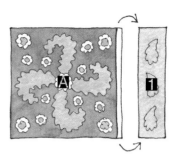

1 When all the quilting is finished, cut away any excess fabric and trim the blocks and central strips to size as follows:
- four feather blocks: 21 x 21 in/53 x 53 cm
- four central strips: 6 x 21 in/15 x 53 cm
- small central flower square: 6 x 6 in/15 x 15 cm

2 From the 17 x 64 in/43 x 163 cm piece of pale blue quilted fabric, cut four borders, two measuring 48 x 3 in/122 x 8 cm, and two measuring 60 x 3 in/152 x 8 cm. Cut identical pieces from the mid-blue quilted piece.

3 All the pieces are now ready to be joined together using the white joining strips. The strips for the front of the quilt are 1 in/3 cm wide and the strips for the back are 1¹/₂ in/4.5 cm wide.

4 Press all the 1¹/₂ in/4.5 cm joining strips in half lengthways, wrong sides together, taking care not to distort the strip as you iron. Measure again to make sure each strip is still the correct length.

5 Working in rows initially, from left to right, and taking a ¹/₄ in/0.75 cm seam allowance every time, join the blocks, white joining strip and pale blue central strips together as follows. Start by joining block A to central strip 1. Align the edge of a 1 x 21 in/ 3 x 53 cm strip with the right edge of block A, right sides together. Pin, easing any fullness. Do not cut away any excess fabric but ease gently to fit.

6 On the back of block A, align the raw edges of a folded 1¹/₂ x 21 in/4.5 x 53 cm strip with the right edge of the block and pin through all the layers, easing to fit as before. Stitch carefully through all the layers.

7 Place the long side of central strip 1, right sides together, against the other side of the 1 x 21 in/3 x 53 cm strip (*diagram 3*). Pin, easing to fit, then stitch. The joining strip at the front should now measure ¹/₂ in/1.5 cm wide. On the back of the block, finger press the folded strip over to meet the seam line on central strip 1 and pin or baste. Slip-stitch with tiny stitches.

8 Block A is now joined to internal strip 1. Repeat the process to attach the right edge of central strip 1 to the left edge of block B (*diagram 4*).

diagram 4

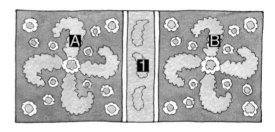

9 Following the same process, carefully attach all the relevant pieces together to make rows C-4-D and 2-E-3, then attach 1 x 48 in/3 x 122 cm joining strips to the front top and bottom of row 2-E-3 (*diagram 5*). Join folded 1¹/₂ x 48 in/4.5 x 122 cm white joining strips to the back top and bottom.

diagram 5

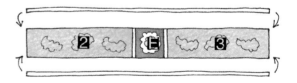

10 Join this piece to rows A-1-B and C-4-D as before to complete the central section of the quilt (*diagram 6*).

diagram 6

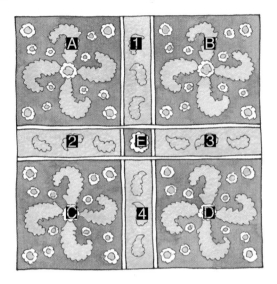

diagram 7

ADDING THE BORDERS

1 Attach the pale blue inner and mid-blue outer borders to the sides of the central section, using four 1 x 48 in/3 x 122 cm joining strips and four folded 1¹/₂ x 48 in/4.5 x 122 cm joining strips. Finish by attaching the pale blue inner and mid-blue outer borders to the top and bottom of the quilt, using the four 1 x 60 in/3 x 152 cm strips and four folded 1¹/₂ x 60 in/4.5 x 152 cm joining strips (*diagram 7*).

2 When all the borders and blocks are assembled, measure the finished quilt. It should measure 60 x 60 in/152 x 152 cm. Use the four white binding strips to bind the edges with a double-fold binding, attaching the two shorter lengths of binding to the sides of the quilt, then using the slightly longer lengths at the top and bottom of the quilt (see Binding the Four Sides Separately on page 17).

9. TUMBLING BLOCKS
Designed by Gail Smith

———

THIS QUILT IS made special by the jewel colors used for the blocks, which are enhanced by the use of black fabric for a dramatic background. When choosing fabrics for the blocks, it is important to pick the correct values – the light, medium and dark shade of each color. Get this right and the clever three-dimensional optical illusion that results will never fail to amaze.

The patchwork employs the piecing-over-papers technique, known as English piecing. The hand stitching required is well worth the effort and has the advantage that much of it can be done while sitting in a comfortable chair.

———

TUMBLING BLOCKS

Quilt Plan

FINISHED SIZE: 41 X 57 ½ IN/96.5 X 135 CM

MATERIALS

All fabrics used in the quilt top are 45 in/115 cm wide, 100% cotton.

Lightweight card stock and printer paper for diamond shapes

Tumbling blocks and pieced border: 15 colored fabrics (i.e. light, medium and dark shades of yellow, purple, blue, red and green), 1/2 yard/40 cm of each

Background, outer border and binding: black marble fabric, 2 1/2 yards/2.3 m

Backing: 1 3/4 yards/1.5 m

Batting: 43 x 60 in/109 x 152 cm black polyester

Thread: yellow, purple, blue, red, green and black cotton for piecing and hand stitching; variegated cotton for quilting

ALTERNATIVE COLOR SCHEMES

1 Paisley prints on a black background.

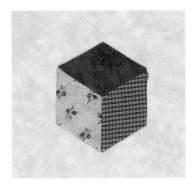

2 Bright and fun red fabrics on a muted background.

3 Pretty mauves.

4 Strong oranges are complemented with darker fabrics.

CUTTING

1 To cut the patchwork tumbling blocks, first make a template of lightweight card stock using the large diamond template on page 109. Using this template and cutting on the straight of grain, cut the following number of diamonds:
  • from each yellow fabric – 10
  • from each purple fabric – 11
  • from each blue fabric – 10
  • from each red fabric – 12
  • from each green fabric – 8

2 Cut 153 diamonds from printer paper, using the smaller diamond template on page 109.

3 From the remaining colored fabric, cut 2 in/5 cm strips, across the width of the fabric, for the pieced inner border.

4 From the black marble fabric, cut a 44 x 60 in/112 x 152 cm rectangle – this will be cut down again later. Cut 10 strips, 2¹/₂ in/6.5 cm deep, across the width of the fabric – five are for the outer border and five are for the binding.

STITCHING

1 First prepare the diamond pieces. Take a paper diamond and a diamond of fabric. Center the paper in the middle of the fabric, on the reverse, and pin in place. Fold the excess fabric over the edge of the paper, making sure you don't fold the paper, and baste in place using a needle and basting thread. Take care at the more acute angles to keep the point sharp. Repeat this process with the remaining paper and fabric diamonds until you have made all 153 diamonds.

2 Now hand stitch the diamonds together in groups of three, taking great care with the orientation of the light, medium and dark diamonds each time. The dark shade should be at the top, the medium on the left and the light on the right – this is the same for all blocks. Start by joining a medium and a light diamond from one color group, stitching them together from the back with a small overstitch or ladder stitch (*diagram 1*).

diagram 1

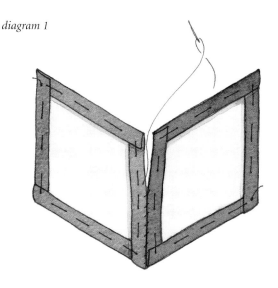

3 Insert a dark-colored diamond on top (*diagram 2*) to complete the hexagonal block.

diagram 2

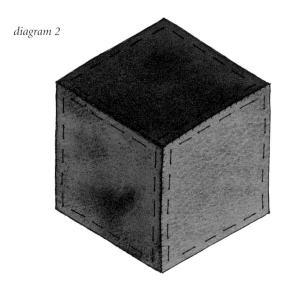

4 Following the quilt plan on page 74, hand stitch hexagons together as required to form two long horizontal block units, each with two rows, and four vertical block units, leaving nine single hexagons.

5 Press the large rectangle of black background fabric. Fold in half lengthways and press down the center to mark a line that will aid positioning of the blocks.

6 Pin one long horizontal block unit to the background fabric, 2 in/5 cm down from the top edge, matching the center of the block with the central line pressed in the background fabric – use a long patchwork ruler to ensure the block is straight. Pin the

other long horizontal block unit at the foot of the quilt, placing it so that the distance between the top of the first block and the top of the second is 37 1/2 in/95 cm.

7 To position the vertical block units, pin the red hexagons at the top of the uppermost blocks 3 in/8 cm beneath the long horizontal block units (measuring from the valley). To position the bottom vertical block units, measure 2 in/5 cm up from the point of the hexagons below. Refer to the quilt plan for the positioning of the remaining single hexagons.

8 Baste these blocks on to the background fabric, basting 1/2 in/1 cm from the edge, then slip-stitch neatly in place using black thread. Keep the work flat if possible at this stage. When you are three-quarters of the way around each hexagon, undo the original basting and slip a finger inside to remove the paper diamonds.

9 Now trim the black fabric to size. Using a patchwork ruler and a pale marking pencil, draw a line 2 in/5 cm away from the side of the hexagons at each side of the quilt. Cut off the excess fabric at the sides. Repeat for the bottom of the quilt. The rectangle should now measure 33 1/2 x 50 in/78.5 x 117 cm – this is important if the pieced border is to fit properly.

ADDING THE BORDERS

1 Taking a 1/4 in/0.75 cm seam allowance, pin and stitch together the colorful 2 in/5 cm strips in order of dark, medium, light in each colorway. Press the strips with all seam allowances going one way, then cross-cut into 2 in/5 cm strips (*diagram 3*).

diagram 3

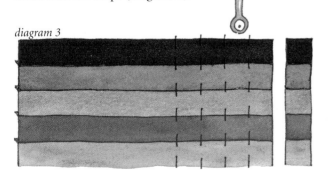

2 Taking the usual seam allowance, stitch the border strips together in the following sequence: blue, green, purple, red and yellow. Prepare border strips like this for the top, sides and bottom of the quilt. With a little planning and adjustment, you should be able to get the sequence to follow but, if you prefer, opt for the random look which is just as effective. Stitch the border strips to the center panel, pressing the seams towards the darker fabric.

3 Join the five black strips for the outer border with diagonal seams to make a continuous length to fit all around the quilt. (For sewing diagonal seams, see page 16, diagram 22.) Taking the usual seam allowance, stitch in place, mitering the corners.

FINISHING

1 Spread the backing right side down on a flat surface, then smooth out the batting and the patchwork top, right side up, centrally on top. Fasten together with safety pins or baste in a grid.

2 Using variegated thread and a walking foot, machine quilt 1/4 in/0.75 cm around the blocks on the black fabric. (See Machine Quilting instructions on page 15.) Sew in any loose ends on the back of the quilt.

3 Join the five black binding strips with diagonal seams to make a continuous length to fit all around the quilt and use to bind the edges with a double-fold binding, mitered at the corners. (See Continuous Strip Binding instructions on page 16.)

10. FANS BY THE CABIN

Designed by Jane Coombes

VIVID BLUES AND LUSCIOUS oranges bring to mind hot days beside the Mediterranean Sea when one may need to be cooled by a fan in the shade of a log cabin! This lap throw quickly comes together using a "quilt as you go" technique in order to allow easy access for the detailed stitching around the appliqué shapes. You will need four shades of orange fabric and five of blue.

FANS BY THE CABIN

Quilt Plan

FINISHED SIZE: 52⅞ X 68⅞ IN/132 X 172 CM

MATERIALS

All fabrics used in the quilt are 42 – 44 in/107 – 115 cm wide, 100% cotton.

Rotary square ruler: $9^1/_2$ in/25 cm

Large central background squares for appliqué: pale orange and pale blue, 1 yard/75 cm of each

Log cabin blocks: light orange and light blue, $^1/_4$ yard/10 cm of each; medium orange and medium blue, $^1/_2$ yard/25 cm of each; dark orange and dark blue, $^1/_2$ yard/40 cm of each

Inner border: medium orange, $^1/_2$ yard/33 cm

Fan appliqué, small patchwork squares, outer border and binding: very dark blue, $2^3/_4$ yards/2.5 m

Appliqué for outer border: light blue, $^1/_2$ yard/40 cm

Paper-backed fusible webbing: $3^1/_2$ yards x 12 in/3.25 x 0.3 m

Backing: $3^1/_3$ yards/3.1 m

Cotton batting: 35 x $8^3/_4$ in/22 cm squares for the blocks; two $2^1/_2$ x $44^1/_2$ in/6.5 x 111.5 cm and two $2^1/_2$ x $56^1/_2$ in/6.5 x 141.5 cm strips for inner border; two $4^1/_2$ x $60^1/_2$ in/11.5 x 151.5 cm and two $4^1/_2$ x $52^1/_2$ in/11.5 x 131.5 cm strips for outer border

Thread: 100% cotton for piecing; royal blue metallic, very dark blue, medium blue, medium orange and light blue machine embroidery threads

ALTERNATIVE COLOR SCHEMES

1 Greens, reds and yellows for a classic look.

2 Soft mauves and pinks for a feminine feel.

3 Contemporary jades and reds for a smart, modern look.

4 Bright and bold – great for a child's bedroom.

CUTTING

1 From the pale orange fabric, cut three strips, 8³/₄ in/ 22 cm deep, across the width of the fabric. Cross-cut these to produce nine 8³/₄ in/22 cm squares. Cut the pale blue fabric in exactly the same way.

2 From both the light orange and the light blue fabric, cut one strip, 1⁷/₈ in/4.8 cm deep, across the width of the fabric.

3 From both the medium orange and the medium blue fabric, cut the following pieces:
- two strips, 1⁷/₈ in/4.8 cm deep, across the width of the fabric. Cross-cut these to produce seventeen 3¹/₈ x 1⁷/₈ in/8.2 x 4.8 cm rectangles.
- one strip, 4¹/₂ in/11.5 cm deep, across the width of the fabric.

From the remaining medium orange fabric cut five strips, 2¹/₂ in/6.5 cm deep, across the width of the fabric, for the inner border.

4 From both the dark orange and the dark blue fabric, cut the following pieces:
- three strips, 1⁷/₈ in/4.8 cm deep, across the width of the fabric. Cross-cut these to produce seventeen 5⁷/₈ x 1⁷/₈ in/14.8 x 4.8 cm rectangles.
- one strip, 7¹/₈ in/18.2 cm deep, across the width of the fabric.

5 From the very dark blue fabric, cut the following pieces:
- six strips, 1⁷/₈ in/4.8 cm deep, across the width of the fabric.
- seven strips, 4¹/₂ in/11.5 cm deep, across the width of the fabric. Cross-cut these to produce fifty-six 4¹/₂ in/11.5 cm squares for the outer border.
- seven strips, 2¹/₄ in/5.75 cm deep, across the width of the fabric, for the binding.

(The remainder of the very dark blue fabric is for the fan appliqué shapes.)

6 From the backing fabric, cut the following pieces:
- nine strips, 8³/₄ in/22 cm deep, across the width of the fabric. Cross-cut these to produce eighteen 8³/₄ in/22 cm squares.

- five strips, 2¹/₂ in/6.5 cm deep, across the width of the fabric, for the inner border.
- six strips, 4¹/₂ in/11.5 cm deep, across the width of the fabric, for the outer border.

WORKING THE APPLIQUÉ

1 Trace the appliqué templates on page 109 on to the paper side of the fusible webbing. You need a total of 72 of each fan shape.

2 Iron the webbing, paper side up, on to the reverse of the remaining very dark blue fabric. Cut out all the shapes and set them aside, putting the 72 pieces of each different shape in separate labeled bags to avoid confusion.

3 Fold and lightly press all the pale orange and pale blue squares on the diagonal twice so as to mark the center of each square.

4 Remove the backing paper from the reverse of the shapes and iron them into position on the right side of the squares. Ensure the points of the "A" shapes are 1¹/₂ in/3.8 cm away from the central point of each square (*diagram 1*). Arrange shapes B, C, D and E accordingly.

diagram 1

5 Using the remaining template on page 109, lightly mark the quilting design (*diagram 2*) on the right side of these appliquéd blocks, taking care to center it between the appliqué shapes.

diagram 2

6 Place a square of backing right side down on a flat surface. Place a square of batting and an appliquéd block, right side up, on top. Pin or baste together through all the layers.

7 Using royal blue metallic machine embroidery thread on the spool and very dark blue thread on the bobbin, machine stitch the quilting design in a continuous line (*diagram 3*).

diagram 3

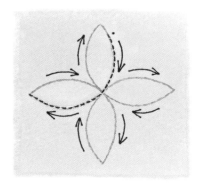

8 Straight machine stitch close to the raw edges of the appliqué shapes, using very dark blue machine embroidery thread on both the spool and the bobbin.

9 Trim the blocks to measure 8¹/₂ in/21.5 cm square.

STITCHING

1 Start constructing the log cabin blocks. With right sides together and taking a ¹/₄ in/0.75 cm seam allowance, pin then stitch together the longest edges of the light orange strip and one of the very dark blue strips. Press the seam allowances towards the very dark blue fabric then cross-cut into 17 units, 1⁷/₈ in/4.8 cm wide (*diagram 4*).

diagram 4

2 Repeat Step 1, this time joining the light blue strip with another of the very dark blue strips.

3 Taking the usual seam allowance, join the units made in Steps 1 and 2 to make 17 four-patch blocks (*diagram 5*). Press the seam allowances to one side.

diagram 5

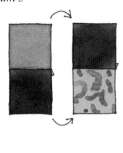

4 Stitch the medium orange and medium blue rectangles to opposite sides of the four-patch blocks (*diagram 6*), again taking the usual seam allowance. Press the seam allowances towards the rectangles.

diagram 6

5 Pin then stitch together the longest edges of the 4¹/₂ in/11.5 cm wide medium orange strip and another of the very dark blue strips. Press the seam allowances away from the very dark blue fabric then cross-cut into 17 units, 1⁷/₈ in/4.8 cm wide (*diagram 7*).

diagram 7

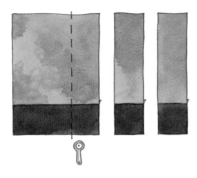

6 Repeat Step 5, this time joining the medium blue strip with another of the very dark blue strips.

7 Referring to *diagram 8* and taking the usual seam allowance, join the units made in Steps 5 and 6 to the partly made blocks from Step 4, noting the position of the very dark blue squares. Press the seam allowances towards the units just added.

8 Attach the dark orange and dark blue rectangles (*diagram 8*) and press the seam allowances towards these rectangles.

diagram 8

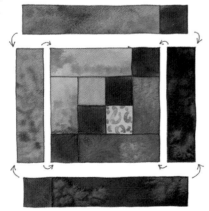

9 Lastly, repeat Steps 5 and 6 to join the dark orange and dark blue strips with the remaining two very dark blue strips. Attach these as per *diagram 8* to complete the 17 log cabin blocks.

10 Place a square of backing right side down on a flat surface. Place a square of batting and a log cabin block, right side up, on top. Pin or baste together through all the layers.

11 Machine quilt in-the-ditch around the very dark blue squares using very dark blue machine embroidery thread. Apply free motion machine quilting over the "logs" using medium blue thread on the blue fabrics and medium orange thread on the orange fabrics. (For these quilting techniques, see page 15.)

12 Trim the blocks to 8¹/₂ in/21.5 cm square.

13 Now join the blocks together. Lay out the blocks according to the quilt plan on page 80, then join them in rows as follows. Taking care to keep the position of each block correct, place one appliquéd block and one log cabin block together, right sides facing. With the wrong side of the appliquéd block facing upwards, fold the unstitched area of the backing fabric away from the batting along the edge to be stitched to the log cabin block. Pin through the remaining five layers of fabric and batting (*diagram 9*).

diagram 9

14 Taking the usual seam allowance and using a walking foot if necessary, machine stitch the layers together. Very carefully trim away as much batting as possible from the seam allowance.

15 Now turn under ¹/₄ in/0.75 cm along the edge of the appliquéd block backing fabric that has just been stitched. Slip-stitch this folded edge to the backing of the log cabin block, just covering the machine stitching but leaving ³/₄ in/2 cm free at each end. Lightly press the seam from both the front and back of the quilt.

16 Repeat Steps 13 to 15 until you have made seven rows of five blocks each.

17 Now join the seven rows together. Note that, even though the loose backing fabric of the appliquéd blocks will alternate on the back of the quilt, you can still stitch the seam in one go.

ADDING THE BORDERS

1 To make the inner border, join the five medium orange strips to make a continuous length. Press the seam allowances open then cut the length into two 44$\frac{1}{2}$ in/111.5 cm long strips and two 56$\frac{1}{2}$ in/141.5 cm long strips.

2 Repeat Step 1 using the five strips of backing fabric.

3 With right sides together, pin the 56$\frac{1}{2}$ in/141.5 cm lengths of orange fabric to either side of the quilt top, and the 56$\frac{1}{2}$ in/141.5 cm lengths of backing fabric to either side of the quilt back.

4 Place the long lengths of batting against the wrong side of the backing fabric strips then reposition the pins to secure all six layers together. Stitch the layers together, taking the usual seam allowance, then very carefully trim away as much batting as possible from the seam allowance.

5 Remove the pins, turn the border and the border backing and batting into position, away from the log cabin and appliquéd blocks, and lightly press from both the front and the back of the quilt.

6 Machine quilt along the border in a straight line, $\frac{1}{4}$ in/0.75 cm away from the seam line using medium orange thread.

7 For the outer border, trace the border appliqué template on page 109 on to the paper side of the fusible webbing. You need a total of 112 shapes. Iron the webbing, paper side up, on to the reverse of the remaining light blue fabric. Cut out the shapes.

8 Fold and lightly press half of the 56 very dark blue squares on the diagonal twice so as to mark the center of each square.

9 Remove the backing paper from the reverse of the appliqué shapes and iron them into position on the right side of the squares. Straight machine stitch close to the raw edges of the appliqué shapes using light blue thread.

10 Referring to the quilt plan on page 80, join eight plain very dark blue squares to seven appliquéd blocks to make one side border strip. Press the seam allowances towards the appliquéd blocks. Repeat.

11 Join seven appliquéd blocks to six plain very dark blue squares to make one top border strip. Press as before. Repeat to make the bottom border strip.

12 Stitch together the six backing fabric strips to make a continuous length. Press the seam allowances open then cut the length into two 52$\frac{1}{2}$ in/131.5 cm long strips and two 60$\frac{1}{2}$ in/151.5 cm long strips.

13 Stitch the border and backing strips to the quilt as you did for the inner border, Steps 3 to 5.

14 Machine quilt a straight line along the inner border, $\frac{1}{4}$ in/0.75 cm away from this seam line using medium orange thread. Apply free motion machine quilting over the plain very dark blue squares in the outer border using very dark blue thread.

FINISHING

1 Join the very dark blue binding strips with diagonal seams to make a continuous length to fit all around the quilt and use to bind the edges with a double-fold binding, mitered at the corners. (See Continuous Strip Binding instructions on page 16.)

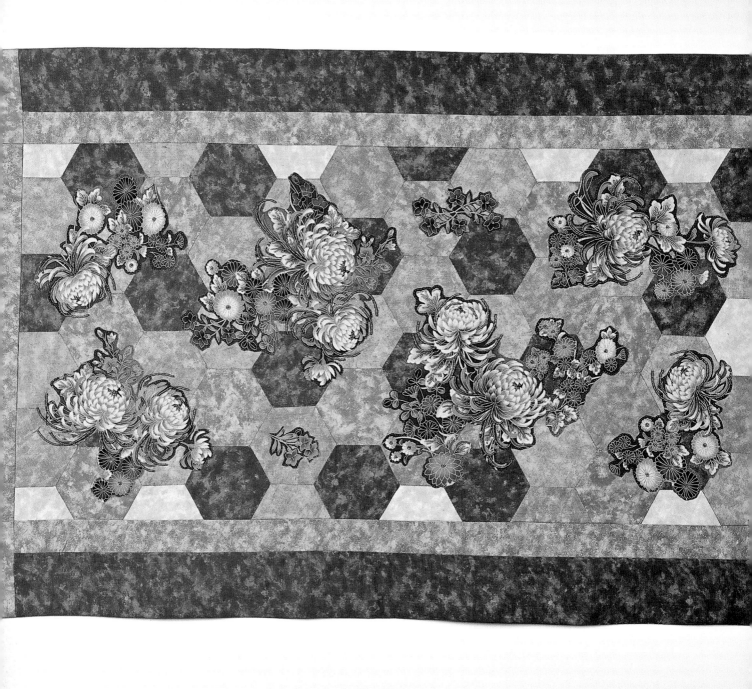

11. BRODERIE PERSE

Designed by Karen Odinga

———

BRODERIE PERSE IS A METHOD, dating from the 18th century, of hand stitching motifs from pre-printed fabric on to a background – in this case a background of patchwork hexagons, created by using the piecing-over-papers technique. Adding bead embroidery gives extra light and texture to the piece. You will need a colorful cotton fabric depicting bold motifs for the broderie perse and five plain batik or marbled cotton fabrics in toning or contrasting colors for the hexagons and borders.

———

BRODERIE PERSE

Quilt Plan

FINISHED SIZE: 30 X 50 IN/74 X 126.5 CM

MATERIALS

All fabrics used in the quilt top are 45 in/115 cm wide, 100% cotton.

Lightweight card stock and freezer paper for hexagonal shapes

Hexagons, inner border and large corner squares: gold, 1 yard/1 m

Hexagons and outer borders: rose, 1 yard/1 cm

Hexagons: tan and mid-green, $1/2$ yard/45.5 cm of each; light green, 1 fat quarter

Motifs and backing: bold patterned print, 2 yards/185 cm (Note: $1/2$ yard/45.5 cm is reserved for cutting out motifs; buy a bit more fabric if the motifs are large)

Paper-backed lightweight fusible webbing: $1/2$ yard/45.5 cm

Lightweight iron-on stabilizer: $1/2$ yard/45.5 cm

Batting: $1 1/2$ yards/1.35 m, lightweight cotton

Thread: neutral silk for hand piecing; medium gold metallic thread for embroidery; neutral beading thread; monofilament transparent thread; quilting cotton to match backing fabric

Beads: 1 oz/30 g size 15 gold beads; $1 1/2$ oz/45 g size 9 or 12 seed beads

---

ALTERNATIVE COLOR SCHEMES

1 Bright and bold.

2 Soft shades for a calming effect.

3 Strong, fresh greens.

4 Spotted fabrics for a quirky feel.

CUTTING

1 Using template A1 or A2 (depending on whether you're working in imperial or metric measurements) from page 109, cut a hexagon template from lightweight card stock. Use this card template to cut 66 hexagonal shapes from freezer paper (widely available from grocery stores and craft shops).

2 Using template B1 or B2 (depending on whether you're working in imperial or metric measurements) from page 109, cut a second template from lightweight card stock. Use this card template to cut 15 hexagons from each of the gold, rose, tan and mid-green fabrics. From the light green fabric, cut six more hexagons using the same template.

3 From the remaining gold fabric, cut four strips, 2 in/5 cm deep, across the width of the fabric, for the inner borders. Cut four $5^{1}/_{2}$ in/13.5 cm squares for the quilt corners.

4 From the remaining rose fabric, cut four strips, 4 in/10 cm deep, across the width of the fabric, for the outer borders.

5 Cut the patterned backing fabric and cotton batting to match the size of the finished quilt top.

STITCHING

1 Before you can start stitching the central panel, first prepare the hexagonal pieces. Iron the freezer paper hexagons (shiny side down) on to the wrong side of the fabric hexagons. Trim the seam allowance to $^{1}/_{4}$ in/ 0.75 cm from the edge of the paper, then press the seam allowance on each side of the hexagons over the edge of the paper to form good, sharp edges.

2 Arrange the hexagons at random to form a rectangle comprising 12 rows of alternately five or six hexagons. Hand stitch neatly together using neutral silk thread. When all the hexagons have been stitched together, peel the freezer paper away from the fabric. Square off any protruding hexagon halves to form the rectangular foundation piece of the quilt.

BRODERIE PERSE AND BEAD EMBROIDERY

1 From the patterned fabric, cut out suitable motifs, leaving a generous $^{1}/_{4}$ in/0.75 cm raw edge around each shape for stitching. Iron the fusible webbing on to the reverse of the motif shapes and trim any excess webbing flush with the fabric edges.

2 Remove the backing paper from the reverse of the motifs and arrange them on the foundation piece of hexagons as desired, then iron in place.

3 Stitch around each motif using gold metallic thread in an even running stitch (*diagram 1*) — use an embroidery hoop for a smooth finish.

diagram 1

4 On the reverse of the patchwork foundation piece, iron a piece of lightweight stabilizer behind each appliquéd motif.

5 Turn the piece to the front again and highlight areas of the motifs with lines of bead embroidery (see Step 6), for example, accent gold print lines on flower stems, centers and petals. Use different sizes of gold beads to create depth and sparkle. For example, stitch small beads on delicate lines or flower centers and stitch larger beads on bolder shapes and lines for stronger impact.

diagram 2

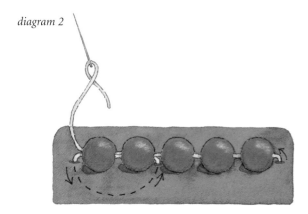

6 To create a durable line of beads, use embroidery backstitch (*diagram 2*). Using a needle threaded with neutral beading thread, come up through the underside of the fabric and string on four or five beads. Keeping the beads taut on the thread, take the needle down into the fabric in front of the line of beads. Come back up right behind the second to the last bead and run the needle back through those last two beads. Repeat the stitch along your design as required. For tight curves, you may need to stitch only one bead at a time to maintain a smooth line. Passing the thread back through the entire line of beads can also further smooth a line of stitched beads. (An embroidery hoop is unnecessary here because the stabilizer backing will keep the fabric stable but still comfortably pliable.)

ADDING THE BORDERS

1 Carefully press the completed foundation section of the quilt, taking care around the bead embroidery. Measure the completed foundation section through the center from side to side, then cut two of the 2 in/5 cm gold strips and two of the 4 in/10 cm rose strips to this measurement.

2 Measure the pieced top through the center from top to bottom, then cut the remaining 2 in/5 cm gold strips and the remaining 4 in/10 cm rose strips to this measurement.

3 Taking a 1/4 in/0.75 cm seam allowance, pin and stitch the four gold strips to the completed foundation section. Apply free motion machine embroidery to the gold inner border using gold metallic thread.

4 Taking the usual seam allowance, pin and stitch the four rose strips to the edges of the quilt top. To the end of each long gold and rose border, pin and stitch a gold 5 1/2 in/13.5 cm square. Pin and stitch the remaining seams to attach the corner squares fully and square off the corners.

5 Embellish each gold corner square with an additional motif from the printed fabric and decorate with bead embroidery as before.

FINISHING

1 Finish the quilt using the "bagging out" method of joining the layers. (See Assembling Where No Binding is Used on page 14.) Spread out the batting on a flat surface. Smooth out the patchwork top, right side up, on top. Place the patterned backing fabric on top, right side down. Pin all around the edges and into the center to secure.

2 Taking the usual seam allowance, stitch around all four sides, leaving an opening along one of the short sides for turning. Trim the batting close to the seam to reduce the bulk on turning but don't trim the fabric seams. Turn the whole quilt the right side out so that the batting is now on the inside. Slip-stitch the opening closed. Lightly press the quilt.

3 Using clear monofilament thread on the spool and a bobbin thread to match the patterned print, machine quilt in-the-ditch along the border seams. (See In-the-Ditch Machine Quilting on page 15.)

4 Using the gold metallic thread, hand stitch small cross-stitches through all three fabric layers on each hexagon corner for a subtle, tied quilted effect.

12. WATERCOLOR SUNFLOWERS

Designed by Nikki Foley

ONE WARM SUNNY DAY in autumn at a country market on the west coast of Ireland, I met a lady who had painted slates with bold images of flowers on a mosaic background. Her work inspired me to make this quilt comprising a pieced watercolor-effect background with bright sunflowers appliquéd on top. When choosing fabrics for the background, try to avoid any that are too heavily patterned.

WATERCOLOR SUNFLOWERS

Quilt Plan

FINISHED SIZE: 45 X 49 IN/112.5 X 122.5 CM

MATERIALS

All fabrics used in the quilt top are 45 in/115 cm wide, 100% cotton. The backing fabric is 60 in/150 cm wide.

Background squares: 18 colored fabrics (light blue, mid-blue, light turquoise, mid-turquoise, pale lilac, mid-lilac, light purple, white with a hint or print of blue, red, orange, yellow, pink, beige, dark beige, light brown, mid-brown, dark brown and red brown), one fat eighth (see tip) of each

Leaves: bright citrus green, 1/4 yard/18 cm

Inner border and binding: black, 3/4 yard/70 cm

Outer border: very dark brown or black print, 1/2 yard/50 cm

Freezer paper: 40 in/102 cm

Sunflower petals: bright yellow, 1/2 yard/50 cm

Sunflower centers: scraps of brown check

Flower pot: brown, one fat quarter

Backing: 1 1/2 yards/ 1.2 m in color of your choice

Batting: 46 x 50 in/115 x 125 cm

Thread: neutral cotton for piecing; colored cotton to match appliqué fabrics; pale blue and yellow for machine quilting; golden yellow embroidery thread for hand quilting

TIP

A "fat eighth" is a term used by fabric suppliers to describe a piece of fabric approximately 22 x 9 in/46 x 23 cm. A "fat quarter" is 22 x 18 in/56 x 50 cm.

ALTERNATIVE COLOR SCHEMES

1 Bright reds against a white background.

2 Mauves in various shades.

3 Strong yellows and blues.

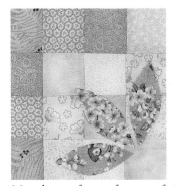

4 Muted tones for a soft, warm feel.

CUTTING

1 Cut all the blue, turquoise, lilac and purple fat eighths (i.e. a total of eight pieces of fabric) into strips, $2^1/_2$ in/6.5 cm wide, along the length of the fabric. Cross-cut all the strips to produce $2^1/_2$ in/6.5 cm squares. You need a total of 148 squares.

2 From the red fabric, cut one strip $2^7/_8$ in/7.5 cm deep, across the width of the fabric. From this strip cross-cut one $2^7/_8$ in/7.5 cm square.

3 From each of the orange, yellow and pink fat eights, cut two strips, $2^7/_8$ in/7.5 cm deep, across the width of the fabric. Cross-cut these strips into $2^7/_8$ in/7.5 cm squares. You need four of each color.

4 From each of the six brown fabrics, cut one strip, $2^7/_8$ in/7.5 cm along the length of the fabric. Cross-cut the strips into $2^7/_8$ in/7.5 cm squares. You need a total of 17 squares.

5 Cut the remaining red, orange, yellow, pink and brown fabrics into $2^1/_2$ in/6.5 cm strips along the length of the fabric, and then cross-cut the strips into $2^1/_2$ in/6.5 cm squares.

6 From the green fabric, cut one $2^7/_8$ x $11^1/_2$ in/7.5 x 30 cm strip. Cross-cut into four $2^7/_8$ in/7.5 cm squares. (The remainder of the fabric is for the appliqué sunflower leaves.)

7 From the black fabric, cut four strips, 3 in/7.75 cm deep, across the width of the fabric, for the inner border. Cut five strips, $2^1/_2$ in/6.5 cm deep, across the width of the fabric, for the binding.

8 From the very dark brown or black print, cut four strips, 4 in/10.25 cm deep, across the width of the fabric, for the outer border.

STITCHING

1 Start by making the half-square triangles. Using a sharp pencil, draw a diagonal line across the wrong side of each of the red, orange, yellow, pink and green $2^7/_8$ in/7.5 cm squares.

2 Place each of these marked squares against one of the 17 brown $2^7/_8$ in/7.5 cm squares, right sides together. Pin then stitch $1/_4$ in/0.75 cm either side of the penciled line. Press as stitched to embed the stitches and to avoid stretching, then carefully cut along the penciled line, open out and press the seam allowances towards the darker fabric.

3 Following the quilt plan on page 94 and *diagram 1*, lay out 288 x $2^1/_2$ in/6.5 cm squares and half-square triangles in 18 rows of 16. Pin and stitch together in rows, taking a $1/_4$ in/0.75 cm seam allowance each time. Press, then stitch the rows together to complete the center panel.

diagram 1

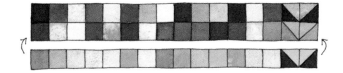

WORKING THE APPLIQUÉ

1 Using the appliqué templates on page 110, trace the large petal template 22 times on to the paper side of the freezer paper. Similarly, trace the small petal template seven times, the small circle template once and large circle template twice. Also trace one flower pot and five leaves. Cut out all the shapes.

2 Iron the large and small petal shapes, shiny side down, on to the reverse of the bright yellow fabric. Leave at least $1/_2$ in/1.5 cm between petals then cut out each petal, allowing for a $1/_4$ in/0.75 cm seam allowance around each shape.

3 Peel the freezer paper off the fabric and replace it, shiny side up, on the wrong side of the fabric in exactly the same position. Pin the paper in place then use the side of the iron to press the seam allowance over on to the freezer paper, easing a little fabric at a time so that it sticks to the paper. Don't worry if the iron touches the surface of the freezer paper – it should not stick to the surface of the iron.

4 Repeat this process with the green fabric and the leaf shapes, the scraps of brown check fabric and the paper circles, and the rich brown fabric and the flower pot shape. Set the pieces aside and avoid overhandling or the paper will come away from the fabric.

5 Referring to *diagram 2*, pin the appliqué flower pot on the pieced background. Secure in place, stitching around the neatened edge using tiny slip-stitches and thread that matches the appliqué fabric. Before completely stitching the flower pot in place, remove the freezer paper. Next pin the first layer of appliqué leaves in place. Start stitching halfway along the leaf shape, again using tiny slip-stitches and matching thread. When you reach the tip of the leaf, add an extra stitch to secure, then tuck under the flap of fabric sticking out from underneath and continue stitching to the other end of the leaf. Again, add an extra stitch to secure, then lift up the unstitched fabric and ease out the freezer paper, before stitching the remaining gap closed. Continue stitching all the leaves and petals in place, remembering to remove the freezer paper as you work.

diagram 2

6 Pin and stitch the last layer of appliqué shapes in place (*diagram 3*) as before, finishing with the flower centers and removing the freezer paper each time.

diagram 3

ADDING THE BORDERS

1 Measure the pieced top through the center from top to bottom, then cut two strips of the black inner border fabric to this measurement and stitch to either side.

2 Measure the pieced top through the center from side to side, then cut two strips of the black inner border fabric to this measurement and stitch to the top and bottom of the quilt.

3 Repeat the process with the four strips of very dark brown or black print for the outer border.

FINISHING

1 Spread the backing right side down on a flat surface, then smooth out the batting and the patchwork top, right side up, centrally on top. Fasten together with safety pins or baste in a grid.

2 Using a walking foot and pale blue thread, machine quilt around the flower pot and sunflowers then machine quilt some wavy lines on the background, about 3-4 in/8-10 cm apart, if liked. Using yellow thread, machine quilt along the inner edge of the "frame" created by the brown pieced strips, then machine quilt in-the-ditch around the edge that meets the black border fabric. Machine quilt on the far side of the black border, $1/2$ in/1.25 cm away from the seam with the next border. (For Machine Quilting instructions, see pages 14–15.) Repeat with the outer border. Using golden yellow embroidery thread, hand quilt around the centers of the sunflowers.

3 Trim off any excess batting and backing.

4 Join the binding strips with diagonal seams to make a continuous length to fit all around the quilt and use to bind the edges with a double-fold binding, mitered at the corners. (See Continuous Strip Binding instructions on page 16.)

13. AUTUMN SHADED SHADOWS

Designed by Janet Goddard

―――――――

THIS RICHLY COLORED AUTUMN quilt will appeal to lovers of both machine piecing and appliqué. The center panel contains small squares in autumnal tones, which are graded to create shaded rows. The surrounding appliqué features vines, autumn leaves and blooms, acorns, fruit and squirrels. The quilt is finished with a pieced border.

―――――――

AUTUMN SHADED SHADOWS

Quilt Plan

FINISHED SIZE: 49¾ X 54¼ IN/121 X 131 CM

MATERIALS

All fabrics used in the quilt top are 45 in/115 cm wide, 100% cotton. The backing fabric is 60 in/ 150 cm wide.

Background: beige print, 1 ⅝ yards/140 cm

Small squares and leaves: five rust-colored fabrics graded from light to dark (e.g. light, light/ medium, medium, medium/dark, dark), ¼ yard/20 cm of each

Small squares, leaves, acorn tops and pears: six gold fabrics graded from light to dark, ¼ yard/20 cm of each

Small squares, leaves and flower centers: six brown fabrics graded light to dark, ¼ yard/20 cm of each

Squirrels and acorn bases: dark brown fabric, ¼ yard/20 cm

Vines, leaves and fruit stems: green print, ½ yard/25 cm

Flowers and apples: red print, ¼ yard/20 cm

Binding: brown floral print, ½ yard/30 cm

Paper-backed fusible webbing: 40 in/102 cm

Backing: gold print, 1 ⅝ yards/ 1.6 m

Batting: 56 x 60 in/142 x 152 cm, 80:20 cotton/polyester

Thread: neutral cotton for piecing; colored cotton to match appliqué fabrics; beige cotton for hand quilting; gold embroidery thread for squirrels' eyes

---

ALTERNATIVE COLOR SCHEMES

1 Pretty reds and pinks.

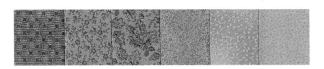

2 Various shades of green bring the outside in.

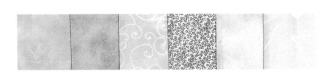

3 Warm and sunny yellows.

4 Bold oranges for a bright and cheery feel.

CUTTING

1 From the beige background print, cut the following pieces from the length of the fabric:
- two $8^1/_2$ x 30 in/22 x 76 cm strips and two $8^1/_2$ x $42^1/_2$ in/22 x 108 cm strips.
- two $3^1/_2$ x $49^1/_2$ in/9 x 126 cm strips and two $3^1/_2$ x 52 in/9 x 132 cm strips.

2 For the squares for the center panel, arrange your fabric from light to dark. Label each fabric with a sticker as you cut. It may be a good idea to cut an extra square of each fabric, stick it to a chart and label it with a number. Label each square with R for rust, G for gold and B for brown followed by a number to represent the shade. The darkest fabric is Number 1 and the lightest is Number 6 (*diagram 1*).

From each of the five rust-colored fabrics, cut twelve 2 in/5 cm squares.

From the six gold fabrics, cut the following number of 2 in/5 cm squares:
- Gold 1 – 28, Gold 2 – 28, Gold 3 – 27, Gold 4 – 26, Gold 5 – 25, Gold 6 – 24

From the six brown fabrics, cut the following number of 2 in/5 cm squares:
- Brown 1 – 16, Brown 2 – 16, Brown 3 – 15
- Brown 4 – 14, Brown 5 – 13, Brown 6 – 12

3 For the squares in the pieced border, cut one-hundred-and-sixteen 2 in/5 cm squares randomly from the remaining rust, gold and brown fabrics left over from cutting the squares for the center panel.

4 From the brown floral print, cut six strips, 2 in/5 cm deep, across the width of the fabric, for the binding.

5 To cut the appliqué shapes, use the appliqué templates on page 111 and trace four vine As, four vine Bs, 24 large leaves, 32 small leaves (roughly half the size of the large leaf), two apples and apple stems, two pears and pear

stems, 16 acorn bases and tops, four flowers, four flower centers and two squirrels on to fusible webbing.

6 Cut out the fused motifs and iron on to the reverse of the appropriate fabric, as follows:
- all eight vines, eight large and eight small leaves, and the apple and pear stems on to the green print.
- the remaining leaves (16 large and 24 small) on to the remaining rust, gold and brown fabrics at random, but ensuring that all fabrics are used.
- 16 acorn bases and two squirrels on to the dark brown fabric.
- four flowers and two apples on to the red print.
- four flower centers on to a remaining light brown fabric.
- 16 acorn tops, two pears and two small nuts on to the remaining gold fabrics.

Cut out all the shapes and set aside.

STITCHING

1 To stitch the center panel, use the placement guide (*diagram 1*) and lay out the first horizontal row of squares. For example R1 indicates the darkest rust-colored fabric while B6 indicates the lightest brown square.

2 Before stitching the first row of squares together double-check that the pieces are in the correct order. When you are satisfied they are correct, stitch the first row together, making sure your $1/_4$ in/0.75 cm seam allowance is accurate.

3 Press the seam allowances in one direction and then label the row (Row 1).

4 Following the quilt plan on page 100, now lay out Row 2 (*diagram 2*). This follows the same order as Row 1 except that the dark red square (R1) is removed

diagram 1

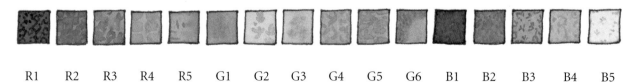

R1   R2   R3   R4   R5   G1   G2   G3   G4   G5   G6   B1   B2   B3   B4   B5

from the left end of the row and set aside and a new light brown square (B6) is added at the right end. Stitch the squares together as in step 2 above. Stitch Rows 1 and 2 together. Press the seam allowances downwards.

diagram 2

	R2	R3	R4	R5	G1	G2	G3	G4	G5	G6	B1	B2	B3	B4	B5	
R2	R3	R4	R5	G1	G2	G3	G4	G5	G6	B1	B2	B3	B4	B5	B6
R3	R4	R5	G1	G2	G3	G4	G5	G6	B1	B2	B3	B4	B5	B6	G1

5 Next lay out Row 3. Use the same order of squares as Row 2 but remove a red square (R2) from the left end and set aside and add a dark gold (G1) to the right. Stitch as before. Stitch Rows 2 and 3 together and press the seam allowances in the opposite direction from Row 2. Continue in this manner until all 19 rows are stitched together, removing and adding colored squares, forming a diagonal pattern as shown in the quilt plan.

WORKING THE APPLIQUÉ

1 To make the appliquéd border, pin then stitch an 8¹/₂ x 30 in/22 x 76 cm beige border strip to each side of the center panel, taking the usual seam allowance. Press the seam allowances towards the border fabric.

2 Pin then stitch the 8¹/₂ x 42¹/₂ in/22 x 108 cm beige border strips to the top and bottom of the center panel. Press the seam allowances towards the border fabric.

3 Now add the appliqué shapes, working on one corner at a time. Remove the backing paper from the reverse of a vine A and a vine B. Position each vine going into the corner. Remove the backing paper from the reverse of a red flower and position the flower diagonally in the corner, ensuring that it covers the end of each vine by ¹/₄ in/0.75 cm (*diagram 3*). Iron in place.

4 Remove the backing paper from the reverse of a brown flower center and position in the middle of the red flower. Iron in place.

diagram 3

5 Repeat this process with the leaves and acorns. Add one large green leaf, one small green leaf, two acorns, two large autumn leaves and three small autumn leaves to each vine, ensuring the leaves all point towards the corner.

6 Repeat this process with all the vines to complete each corner of the quilt.

7 When all four corners have been completed, add the apples and their stems to the top center of the quilt and the pears and their stems to the bottom of the quilt, making sure that the fruit overlaps the ends of the vines. Lastly, place a squirrel and nut in the gap between the vines on each side of the quilt.

8 Zigzag stitch around each shape, matching the thread to the fabric.

9 Using the gold embroidery thread, stitch a French knot on each squirrel's head to represent its eye.

ADDING THE BORDERS

1 To make the pieced border, stitch the remaining 2 in/5 cm squares together into four strips of 29 squares each, taking the usual seam allowance. Make sure the colors are randomly placed so that there is an equal distribution of rust, gold and brown fabrics. Press all seam allowances in each strip in one direction.

2 Stitch a strip to each side of the quilt and press the seam allowances towards the appliquéd border.

3 Stitch a strip to the top and bottom of the quilt and press the seam allowances towards the appliquéd background.

4 For the final border, stitch the 3$^{1}/_{2}$ x 49$^{1}/_{2}$ in/9 x 126 cm strips of beige background fabric to each side of the quilt. Press the seam allowances towards the background fabric.

5 Stitch the 3$^{1}/_{2}$ x 52 in/9 x 132 cm strips of beige background fabric to the top and bottom of the quilt. Press the seam allowances towards the background fabric.

FINISHING

1 Spread the backing right side down on a flat surface, then smooth out the batting and the patchwork top, right side up, centrally on top. Fasten together with safety pins or baste in a grid.

2 Use the leaf quilting template on page 111 to mark leaves over the center panel in a random fashion. Using the beige quilting thread, hand quilt these leaves over the center panel. (For Hand Quilting instructions, see page 15.)

3 Hand quilt $^{1}/_{4}$ in/0.75 cm around each appliquéd shape. Quilt $^{1}/_{4}$ in/0.75 cm in from the seam lines on each side of the beige border strips so that the quilting lies on the beige fabric.

4 Use the acorn quilting template on page 111 to mark acorns randomly on the outer border. Hand quilt each acorn.

5 Trim any excess batting and backing even with the quilt top.

6 Join the binding strips with diagonal seams to make a continuous length to fit all around the quilt and use to bind the edges with a double-fold binding, mitered at the corners. (See Continuous Strip Binding instructions on page 16.)

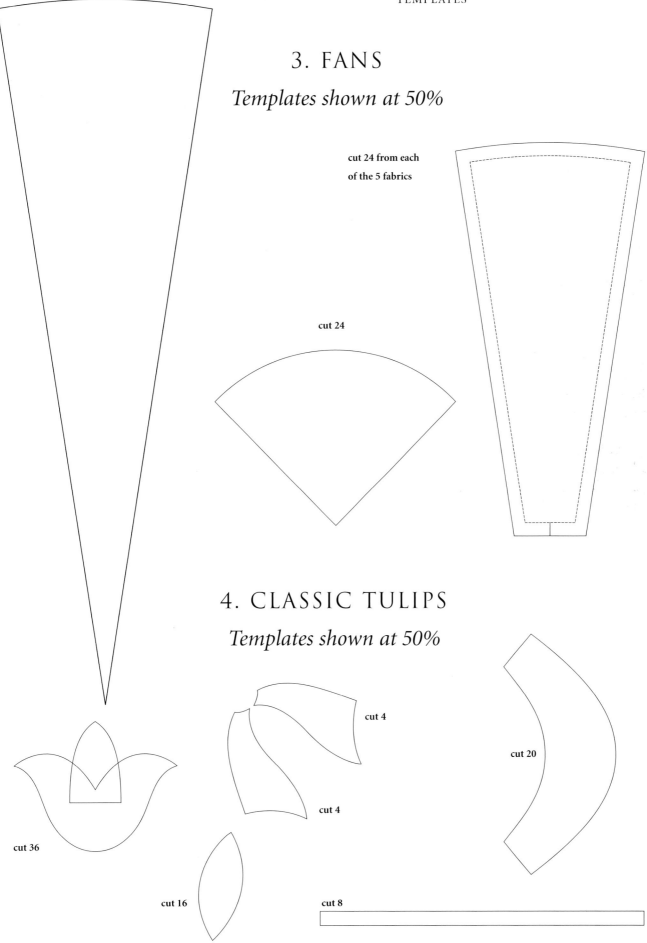

3. FANS
Templates shown at 50%

cut 24 from each
of the 5 fabrics

cut 24

4. CLASSIC TULIPS
Templates shown at 50%

cut 4

cut 20

cut 4

cut 36

cut 16

cut 8

5. QUERCUS AUTUMNALIS

Templates shown at 50%

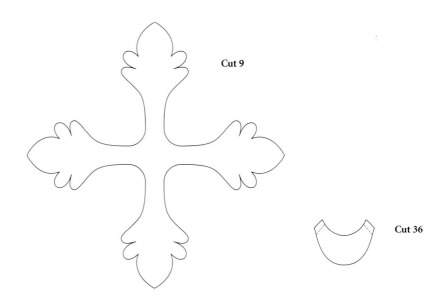

Cut 9

Cut 36

6. TWIRLING ROSE OF SHARON

Templates shown at 50%

1-4 and 12-14 cut 48 of each
5-8 cut 16 of each
9-11 cut 58 of each
15 cut 208

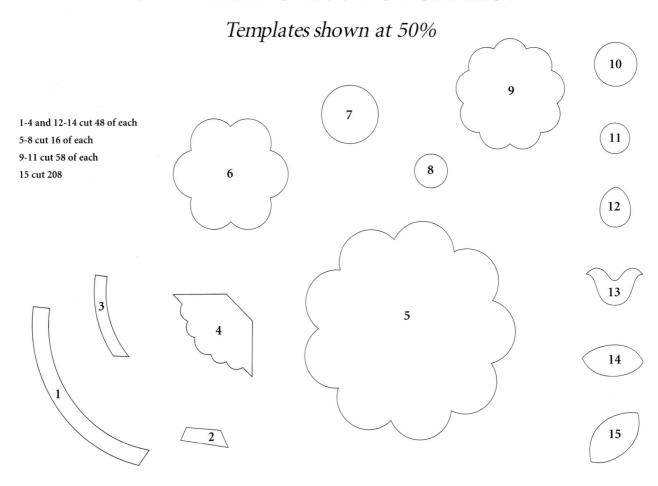

VINE LEAF
for horizontal and outer vertical borders

VINE LEAF
for 12" vertical sashing strips

7. BLOOMS, BASKETS AND BLUEBIRDS
Templates shown at 50%

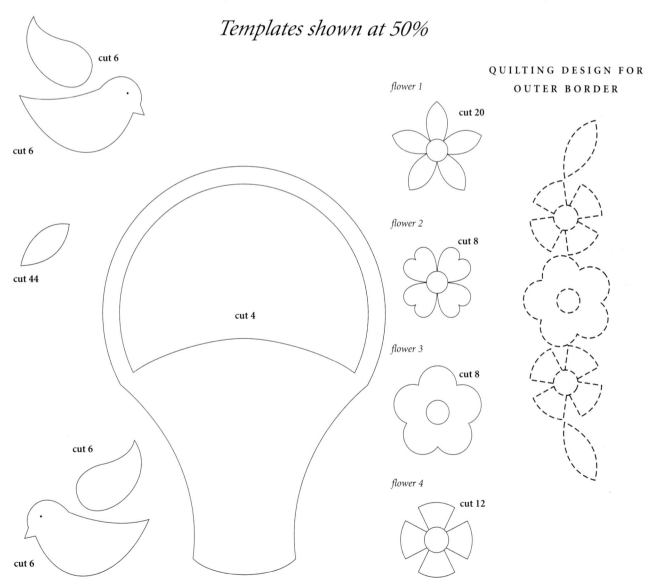

cut 6

cut 6

cut 44

cut 6

cut 6

cut 4

flower 1

cut 20

flower 2

cut 8

flower 3

cut 8

flower 4

cut 12

QUILTING DESIGN FOR
OUTER BORDER

8. PRINCESS FEATHER

Templates shown at 50%

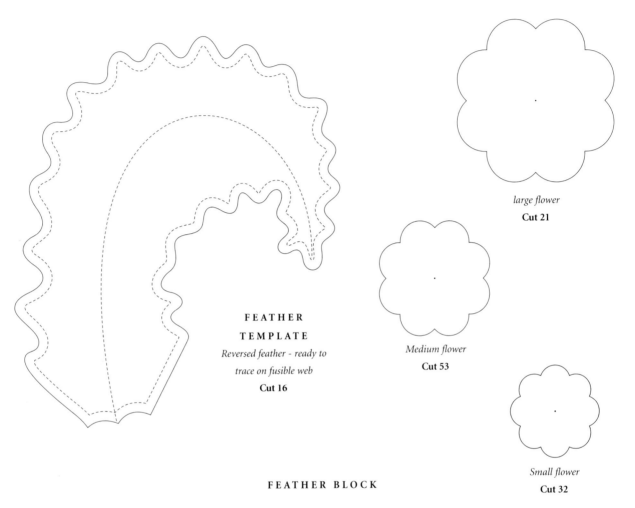

large flower
Cut 21

Medium flower
Cut 53

Small flower
Cut 32

**FEATHER
TEMPLATE**

*Reversed feather - ready to
trace on fusible web*
Cut 16

FEATHER BLOCK

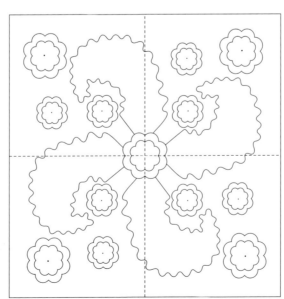

9. TUMBLING BLOCKS

Template shown at 50%

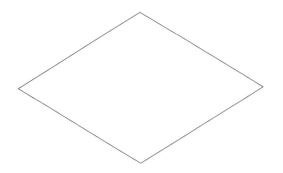

11. BRODERIE PERSE

Templates shown at 50%

10. FANS BY THE CABIN

Templates shown at 50%

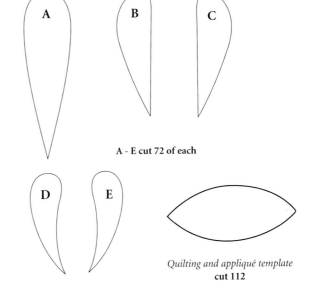

A - E cut 72 of each

Quilting and appliqué template
cut 112

B1
(imperial)

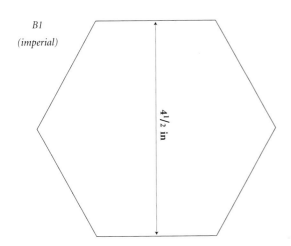

4$\frac{1}{2}$ in

B2
(metric)

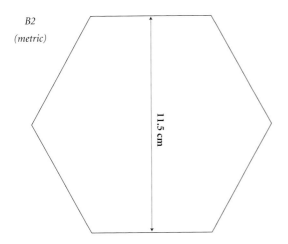

11.5 cm

A1
(imperial)

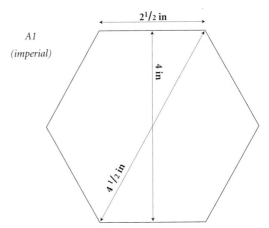

2$\frac{1}{2}$ in

4 in

4 $\frac{1}{2}$ in

A2
(metric)

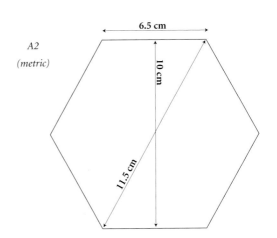

6.5 cm

10 cm

11.5 cm

12. WATERCOLOR SUNFLOWERS

Templates shown at 50%

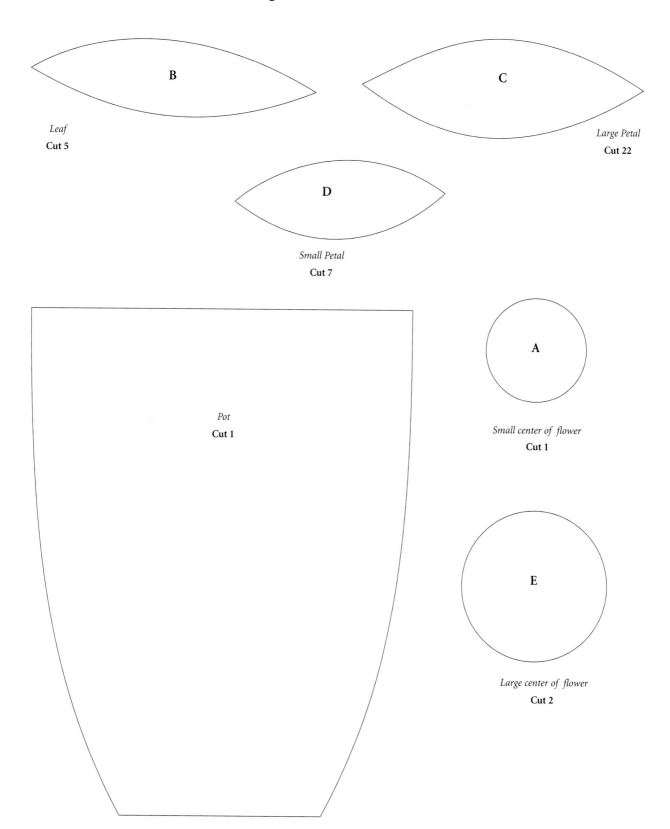

Leaf
Cut 5

Large Petal
Cut 22

Small Petal
Cut 7

Pot
Cut 1

Small center of flower
Cut 1

Large center of flower
Cut 2

13. AUTUMN SHADED SHADOWS

Templates shown at 50%

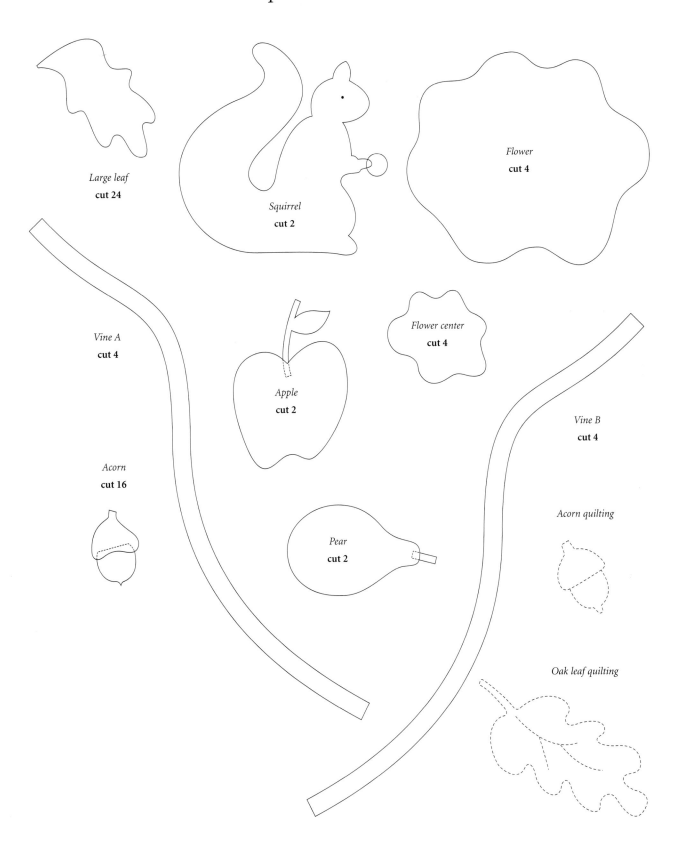

Large leaf
cut 24

Squirrel
cut 2

Flower
cut 4

Vine A
cut 4

Apple
cut 2

Flower center
cut 4

Vine B
cut 4

Acorn
cut 16

Acorn quilting

Pear
cut 2

Oak leaf quilting

INDEX